LUCENT LIBRARY *of* HISTORICAL ERAS

THE INDUSTRIAL REVOLUTION IN BRITAIN

Titles in the series include:

The Industrial Revolution: Social and Economic Effects

The Industrial Revolution in the United States

The Industrial Revolution's Workers and Their Lives

LUCENT LIBRARY ‹of› HISTORICAL ERAS

THE INDUSTRIAL REVOLUTION IN BRITAIN

DON NARDO

LUCENT BOOKS

A part of Gale, Cengage Learning

GALE
CENGAGE Learning·

Detroit • New York • San Francisco • New Haven, Conn • Waterville, Maine • London

GALE
CENGAGE Learning™

LIBRARY OF CONGRESS CATALOGING-IN-PUBLICATION DATA

Nardo, Don, 1947-
  The industrial revolution in Britain / By Don Nardo.
     p. cm. -- (The Lucent library of historical eras)
  Includes bibliographical references and index.
  ISBN 978-1-4205-0152-0 (hardcover)
  1. Industrial revolution--Great Britain--Juvenile literature. 2. Great Britain--Economic conditions--1760-1860--Juvenile literature. I. Title.
  HC254.5.N37 2009
  330.941'07--dc22
                                                                        2008051291

Lucent Books
27500 Drake Rd.
Farmington Hills, MI 48331

ISBN-13: 978-1-4205-0152-0
ISBN-10: 1-4205-0152-6

Printed in the United States of America
1 2 3 4 5 6 7 13 12 11 10 09

Contents

Foreword 6

Introduction
Why Eighteenth-Century Britain? 8

Chapter One
The Rise of Industrial Britain 14

Chapter Two
Textiles Lead the Way 23

Chapter Three
Coal, Iron, and Steel 33

Chapter Four
The Mainspring of Industry: Steam 43

Chapter Five
Transportation and Communications 53

Chapter Six
The Impact of Industrialization 62

Chapter Seven
A Host of Engineering Marvels 72

Epilogue
The Decline of British Industry 83

Notes 87
Time Line 90
For More Information 92
Index 94
Picture Credits 96
About the Author 96

Foreword

Looking back from the vantage point of the present, history can be viewed as a myriad of intertwining roads paved by human events. Some paths stand out—broad highways whose mileposts, even from a distance of centuries, are clear. The events that propelled the rise to power of Germany's Third Reich, its role in World War II, and its eventual demise, for example, are well defined and documented.

Other roads are less distinct, their route sometimes hidden from view. Modern legislatures may have developed from old tribal councils, for example, but the links between them are indistinct in places, open to discussion and interpretation.

The architecture of civilization—law, religion, art, science, and government—as well as the more everyday aspects of our culture—what we eat, what we wear—all developed along the historical roads and byways. In that progression can be traced every facet of modern life.

A broad look back along these roads reveals that many paths—though of vastly different character—seem to converge at a few critical junctions. These intersections are those great historical eras that echo over the long, steady course of human history, extending beyond the past and into the present.

These epic periods of time are the focus of Historical Eras. They shine through the mists of history like beacons, illuminated by a burst of creativity that propels events forward—so bright that we, from thousands of years away, can clearly see the chain of events leading to the present.

Each Historical Eras consists of a set of books that highlight various aspects of these major eras. For example, the Elizabethan England library features volumes on Queen Elizabeth I and her court, Elizabethan theater, the great playwrights, and everyday life in Elizabethan London.

The mini-library approach allows for the division of each era into its most significant and most interesting parts and the exploration of those parts in depth. Also, social and cultural trends as well as illustrative documents and eyewitness accounts can be prominently featured in individual volumes.

Historical Eras presents a wealth of information to young readers. The lively narrative, fully documented primary and secondary source quotations, maps, photographs, sidebars, and annotated bibliographies serve as launching points for class discussion and further research.

In studying the great historical eras, students also develop a better understanding of our own times. What we learn from the past and how we apply it in the present may shape the future and may determine whether our era will be a guiding light to those traveling future roads.

 Introduction

WHY EIGHTEENTH-CENTURY BRITAIN?

Among the various historical eras and movements in the saga of human civilization, the Industrial Revolution that began in the mid- to late 1700s is one of the most important, influential, and often discussed. The word *Industrial* is key to identifying and understanding it. In simple terms, the Industrial Revolution was a major shift in national economies from dependence on agriculture to large-scale exploitation of machines and manufactured goods. Before the revolution most people lived in rural areas and sustained themselves by working the land. During the course of the Industrial Revolution, which lasted until about 1900, huge numbers of people moved into the cities, which grew rapidly. There, they found jobs in newly built factories and in shops that sold the goods made in the factories.

It is significant that the Industrial Revolution did not occur everywhere and at the same time. In fact, in some of the world's poorer countries it has still not taken place to any significant extent. Britain was the birthplace of large-scale industry. That nation (and its empire) led the way in technology, inventions, and their use in manufacturing, transportation, and engineering. Later, in the 1800s, the Industrial Revolution spread to other countries, notably France, Germany, and the United States. In the second half of the nineteenth century, the United States emerged as the world's leading industrial nation. The rise of industry in Britain in the 1700s is often called the "First Industrial Revolution"; the great surge of industry and manufacturing in the United States from the 1860s on is frequently called the "Second Industrial Revolution."

The Earliest Scientists and Machines

The fact that large-scale industrialization first appeared, took hold, and prospered in one particular place at a specific time in history raises an intriguing question that scholars have long debated. Why did it happen in Britain in the 1700s? Put another way, one could ask: Why did an Industrial Revolution not happen in another part of the world in an earlier age?

These questions would be easier to answer if science, technology, and machines had appeared for the first time in Britain in early modern times. However, experts have long recognized that this was not the case. In fact, both the study of science and the first complex machines appeared in Greece between the sixth and first centuries B.C.

The Greek thinkers Anaxagoras, Democritus, Plato, Aristotle, Strabo, and Archimedes, among others, established nearly all of the major scientific sub-disciplines known today. These include astronomy and cosmology, physics and atomic theory, mathematics, biology and botany, medicine, and mechanics (the basis of machines).

In the realm of mechanics, Greek inventors were no less brilliant than their eighteenth-century British counterparts. Archimedes of Syracuse (third century B.C.) created a mechanical apparatus that allowed a single person to move a fully loaded merchant ship using only his own muscle power. Later, Ctesibius (tee-SIB-ee-us) invented the cylinder and plunger, the basis for later devices such as the cylinders and pistons in modern automobile engines. He also designed a water pump that removed water that had leaked into underground mines. And in the first century B.C Hero (or Heron) of Alexandria built the world's first steam engine. It consisted of a hollow metal ball suspended above a pot of boiling water. Steam from the water caused the ball to spin and for any objects connected to the ball to move.

Hero of Alexandria designed a steam engine in the first century B.C., where a ball was placed above a pot of boiling water causing the ball to spin and any objects attached to it to move.

THE GRECIAN IDEA OF THE STEAM-ENGINE.

Limited by Entrenched Tradition

For reasons that are unclear, Hero used his steam engine strictly to make miniature figures and other toys move. He did not apply its principle to large-scale machines that could do useful work. Why did he and other Greek inventors and machinists not use their breakthrough ideas to develop laborsaving devices like those that developed centuries later in Britain?

First, the metalworking techniques of Ctesibius's and Hero's day were primitive by modern standards. No one knew how to make metal machine parts that were both uniform in size and strong enough to withstand great pressure and wear. This limited the size and efficiency of most machines. Thus, Ctesibius was able to design a huge catapult with cylinders and pistons capable of hurling large missiles more than a mile. But the technology to build the device did not exist; so it remained nothing more than a brilliant idea.

Still, it might be argued that, given enough time and money, ancient Greek inventors might have overcome such technical difficulties. They could not, however, overcome larger and deeply entrenched social customs, conditions, and traditions that worked against the development of large-scale industry.

An Ancient Water Pump

The ancient Greek inventor Ctesibius (tee-SIB-ee-us) fashioned a mirror that slid up and down like a window in a sash. The mirror's counterweight was a lead ball that moved up and down inside a tube. This gave Ctesibius the idea for the simple cylinder and plunger, the basis for those used in many modern machines, including car engines. He applied the idea to a pump intended to raise water in mines. The first-century B.C. Roman architect Vitruvius describes the device this way:

It is [made] of bronze. The lower part consists of two similar cylinders at a small distance apart, with outlet pipes. These pipes converge like the prongs of a fork, and meet in a vessel placed in the middle. In this vessel valves [are] accurately fitted above the top openings of the pipes. And the valves, by closing the mouths of the pipes, retain what has been forced by air into the vessel. Above the vessel a cover like an inverted funnel is fitted and attached by a pin. . . . Pistons are now inserted from above and well oiled. Being thus enclosed in the cylinder, they are worked with piston rods and levers.

Vitruvius, *On Architecture*, vol. 2, trans. Frank Granger. Cambridge, MA: Harvard University Press, 2004, p. 311.

The most important among these traditions was the institution of slavery (practiced in all ancient societies, not just Greece). Except for their upkeep, which was minimal, slaves did not have to be paid; so most manual labor was free. And most citizens, especially those in the wealthy ruling classes, saw no need to invest money and effort in work-saving machines. As a result, many people looked on work, particularly menial labor, with contempt. Such attitudes discouraged serious mechanical innovation.

Pursuing Their Mechanical Dreams

In eighteenth-century Britain, by contrast, no entrenched slavery system existed. (Before 1772, when slavery became unlawful in England, a few people did have slaves as domestic servants. But they were few in number and played no significant role in the country's workforce.) Most British therefore saw work, including the menial kind, as necessary and expected. The British attitude toward work was also affected by Britain's rapidly rising population in the 1700s and 1800s. More jobs were needed to sustain more people, many of whom were willing to move anywhere, at any time, to find work. Such an idea was alien to the ancient Greeks in their tiny, self-sufficient city-states in which most labor was done by slaves.

The emergence of many new workers in Britain also coincided with an important ongoing social change that began in the late 1600s and early 1700s. This trend witnessed large numbers of people working harder, but not simply to make ends meet as had been the case in the past. The new availability of a wide range of goods from Britain's overseas colonies was partly responsible for an increased demand for luxury items or goods that would increase one's standard of living. This created more incentive for inventors to find ways of making these goods both in larger quantities and more cheaply.

At the same time, the British government expanded the patent system it had established in the prior century. A patent is a government grant giving an inventor sole rights to his or her idea or device and any monies it might generate. This notion was also unheard of in ancient times. The ability to patent and benefit from their ideas made inventors feel more secure. And they pursued their mechanical dreams with great vigor.

Other factors made mass industrialization possible. As the late American economic historian W.W. Rostow argued, Britain had more ships than other nations. This enabled it to create more wide-ranging markets for its products. It also had abundant natural resources, including coal and iron, both essential to industry. In addition, Britain had a political system in which a parliament (made up of representatives of the people) ran the government. This made it easier than in absolute monarchies like France for businesspeople to influence

1728 — MATTHEW BOULTON — 1809
1736 — JAMES WATT — 1819
1754 — WILLIAM MURDOCH — 1839

The bronze statue by William Bloye, known as The Golden Boys, *stands in Birmingham, England. Left to right is Matthew Boulton, James Watt, and William Murdoch, pioneering inventors and engineers of the Industrial Revolution.*

the government and allowed the development of new economic enterprises. Because of these factors, Rostow says, "Britain alone was in a position to weave together cotton manufacture, coal and iron technology, the steam engine, and ample foreign trade to pull [the Industrial Revolution] off."[1]

Thus, people in ancient times were no less intelligent and inventive than their modern counterparts. And large-scale industry and manufacturing might well have begun in almost any age had the right social and political conditions and attitudes been present. In such a scenario, the history of the world would surely have been very different. As it happened, however, all of the right factors came together for the first time in Britain in the eighteenth century. And that is where the incredible story of the Industrial Revolution begins.

Chapter One

THE RISE OF
INDUSTRIAL BRITAIN

The late 1700s and the first half of the nineteenth century witnessed the momentous transformation of Britain's economy from one based on agriculture to one based mainly on manufacturing. It happened primarily as a result of the introduction of machines and factories that made the relatively inexpensive mass production of many commodities possible. This huge physical and economic change and how it came about is the single most important aspect of the Industrial Revolution in Britain.

Before examining it in detail, however, two other aspects of this so-called revolution must be stressed. First, despite the word "revolution," which usually describes sudden change, the British Industrial Revolution did not happen all at once. Rather, it occurred gradually over the course of several decades. In fact, most people were, for a long time, blissfully unaware of the degree to which machines and the factory system were permanently changing their way of life. "Only around 1830," scholar Kenneth O. Morgan points out, "were people conscious of substantial and permanent industrial change."[2]

Yet once this realization had set in, many people were pleased that their nation had taken the lead in the new machine age. In 1829 the *Edinburgh Review* boasted, "We move mountains, and make seas our smooth highway. Nothing can resist us. We war with rude nature. And by our restless engines, come off always victorious and loaded with spoils."[3]

Another crucial fact about the British Industrial Revolution is that many, if not most, of the machines and other innovations it produced were not completely new ideas that sprang suddenly into the minds of inventors. Indeed, in each stage of industrialization inventors, machinists, and engineers more often than not built upon ideas or inventions of the past. So a great deal of experimentation and development and modification of older ideas occurred with only a minimum of sudden, brilliant inspiration. As a noted expert on the Industrial Revolution, T.S. Ashton, puts it:

> Most discoveries [during the Revolution were] achieved only after repeated trial and error. Many involve[d] two or more previously independent ideas or processes. . . . In this way, for example, [the] iron rail, which had long been in use in

the coal mine, was joined to the locomotive to create the railway.[4]

Transforming Traditional Agriculture

The first major example of this trend of modifying what had come before was a transformation of agriculture in England and other parts of Britain. (In the eighteenth century Britain encompassed England, Wales, and Scotland; Ireland was added in 1801.) Before the Industrial Revolution, most people in Britain and other parts of Europe—around 90 percent of the population—lived in rural areas and sustained themselves by growing crops or raising animals. A majority were poor or nearly so and paid rent

The "Good Old Days" Before Industry

In a book published in 1836, English surgeon Peter Gaskell, a keen observer of the ongoing process of industrialization, looked back with a touch of nostalgia at the preindustrial period, in which most people were involved to some degree in handmade domestic manufacturing. His conception of the benefits of the "good old days" was somewhat exaggerated; most of the preindustrial peasants were very poor, and few of them lived as "comfortably" as he imagined.

These were, undoubtedly, the golden times of manufactures. . . . By all

the processes being carried on under a man's own roof, he retained his individual respectability, he was kept apart from associations that might injure his moral worth, and he generally earned wages which were not only sufficient to live comfortably upon, but which enabled him to rent a few acres of land. . . . It gave him employment of a healthy character and raised him a step in the scale of society above the mere laborer.

Peter Gaskell, *Artisans and Machinery*. London: John W. Parker, 1836, pp. 12–14.

(either money or crops) to a few wealthy landowners. These country folk were the first to feel the effects of mechanization, even before large-scale industry emerged.

Prior to the coming of industrialization, almost all agricultural work was accomplished by people, draft animals, or rudimentary equipment wielded or pulled by them. Thus, to till the soil people either used hoes, which was back-breaking work, or guided a simple plow pulled by an ox, donkey, or horse. The key point here is that nearly all work was done by hand. Scholar Peter N. Stearns writes:

> Except for waterwheels, used mainly to mill grain, almost all tools were designed for manual use. Animals often pulled plows for farming, but planting and harvesting were done by hand, with workers aided by simple tools like sickles. Looms for weaving cloth were powered by foot pedals, and the fibers strung by hand.[5]

Doing such work by hand was not only exhausting and tedious, it could also be inefficient and wasteful. Planting seeds to grow crops was a prevalent example. When people spread seeds by hand, the seeds landed on the ground unevenly, with some entering the furrows the plow had dug and others missing the furrows. Some farmers did not even plow first; they broke up the earth a little with hoes, then spread the seeds, knowing that only some would take hold and germinate. Birds usually ate the wasted seeds.

This and many other traditional aspects of British agriculture changed significantly in the late 1700s and early 1800s thanks to a combination of several factors. One of these was the introduction of new inventions that began to mechanize farming. For instance, Jethro Tull (1674–1741) introduced the seed drill, a simple but ingenious machine mounted on four wooden wheels and pulled along by a horse. A plowlike device attached to the front drilled a hole of a set depth. Then a rotating device dropped in some seeds. Finally, a device mounted on the back of the machine covered the hole with dirt. Very little seed was wasted, and the result was that more crops grew in a field than had grown there under the planting-by-hand system. Widespread use of Tull's seed drill did not occur until decades after his death. But in time it and other machines or machine-made devices greatly increased crop yields, thereby transforming agriculture in Britain. Among them were improved iron plows and a mechanical threshing machine that separated wheat husks from wheat grains easier and faster than before.

However, experts point out that new mechanical inventions played only a small part in Britain's agricultural revolution. Another major factor was "enclosure." In the eighteenth century and early nineteenth century, most plots of farmland in Britain, which before had been part of large open fields, were enclosed by fences. For a variety of reasons, this made

Jethro Tull created the seed drill in the early 1700s. It was pulled by a horse and had a device that dropped seeds and then covered them with dirt, resulting in little seed loss and increased crop yield.

growing crops and raising livestock more efficient. At the same time, new and more efficient crop rotation methods and fertilizers were adopted, and many new fields were created by cutting down forests.

Changes in Work and Labor

One important result of all of these new farming inventions, methods, and developments was that it took fewer workers to do a certain amount work. For example, a field that before took twenty people two weeks to harvest by hand might now, with new machines and methods, require only five people three days to harvest. This had mixed results. On the positive side, more food could be grown more efficiently and more cheaply, and the surplus could feed and support a larger population. But on the negative side, at the same time that Britain's population was rising many agricultural workers lost their jobs. In search of work, large numbers migrated into the cities. Some took jobs in factories, which were expanding because new machines were also transforming industry and manufacturing. English scholar Mark Overton summarizes it this way:

Each agricultural worker produced more food, so the proportion of the workforce in agriculture fell. This

Benefits of Agricultural Advances

Manhattan College scholar Jeff Horn, an authority on the Industrial Revolution, here describes some of the economic and social effects of Britain's agricultural revolution in the 1700s. He emphasizes how that revolution made the age of industry possible.

The production of more grain permitted urban areas to grow. Improved techniques meant that less labor was needed for agriculture. A greater percentage of the population could now labor in industry. By increasing [crop] yields, farmers made more money, which enabled them to purchase manufactured goods. The production of more food allowed prices to fall despite the increasing population. Declining food prices also meant that people could eat more. The decline in the number of stillborn children and in infant mortality is powerful evidence of improved nutrition. Escalating landlord profits that were generated by commercial agriculture could be invested in industry. In short, without the capital [money] and other improvements provided by the agricultural revolution, the Industrial Revolution would not have taken place when or where it did.

Jeff Horn, *The Industrial Revolution.* Westport, CT: Greenwood, 2007, pp. 11–12.

The plow revolutionized agriculture in Britain because farmers were able to plant more seeds at a faster rate and therefore produce a higher yield of crops.

falling proportion of workers in agriculture enabled the proportion working in industry and services to rise. In other words, improved agricultural production made the Industrial Revolution possible. . . . By 1850 only 22 percent of the British workforce was in agriculture [compared with 90 percent in 1700]; [this was] the smallest proportion for any country in the world.[6]

Such changes in the makeup and distribution of the workforce were inevitable. Inventors and engineers had begun to apply their ingenuity and innovation to agriculture, and the results had been impressive. At the same time, they were doing the same thing on a bigger scale in industry by introducing increasingly sophisticated machines to manufacturing and other industries. The areas most affected by mechanization were textiles (spinning, weaving, and clothes making), coal mining, metallurgy (especially the production of iron and products made from iron), and transportation (which was hugely transformed by railroads).

Some of these industries, such as textiles and metallurgy, had existed for centuries. But they had been on a small scale and highly labor intensive. Goods such as clothes, pottery, candles, metal tools and weapons, and so forth had been made almost entirely by hand either in homes or in workrooms run by merchants and other businessmen. These workrooms, which usually employed from three or four to twenty or so workers, were in a sense the first factories.

As this by-hand manufacturing system steadily gave way to machine manufacturing in the late 1700s and early 1800s, the manner in which each laborer approached his or her work also changed. Traditionally, someone working at home or in a workroom accomplished most or all of a manufacturing process him- or herself. For example, a single person often spun some yarn, wove it into cloth, and then cut and sewed the cloth into a piece of clothing. Using this approach, it could take most of or even an entire day to make one shirt or pair of trousers.

But as industrialization increased, the number of workers in factories also increased. Moreover, they became more specialized, with each worker (or group of workers) doing only one part of the process. This became known as division of labor. In his groundbreaking book *The Wealth of Nations*, published in 1776, Scottish philosopher and economist Adam Smith explains and encourages this new system. He provides the now famous example of a factory that manufactured pins (like those used in sewing). He points out that making a pin then required "about eighteen distinct operations," or steps, and when one person tried to do them all it was very slow and inefficient. In contrast, dividing the steps among ten specialized laborers allowed the factory to produce many more pins in a given time span. These workers "could make among them upwards of forty-eight thousand pins in a day," Smith writes.

Each person, therefore, making a tenth part of forty-eight thousand pins, might be considered as making four thousand eight hundred pins in a day. But if they had all wrought [worked] separately and independently, and without any of them having been educated to this peculiar business, they certainly could not each of them have made twenty, perhaps not one pin in a day.[7]

The Power of Industrial Britain

Thus, it was not only technological (or mechanical) advances but also a major reorganization of production processes that drove Britain's Industrial Revolution. This potent combination created vast increases in production output across England and other parts of Britain. Typical was the increase in output of workers in the spinning industry. In 1820, using steam-driven spindles, one of them could make about a hundred times as much thread as he or she could have in preindustrial times. Overall, industrial production in Britain more than doubled each year between 1780 and 1800. And by 1815 Britain produced fully half of all the world's manufactured goods.

For decades this tremendous industrial expansion happened mainly in England with lesser, though still considerable, industrial activity in Scotland and Wales. As with other aspects of the Industrial Revolution, the pattern of emerging industrial towns was in large degree built on patterns of the past. With a few exceptions, mechanized factories were most common in villages and towns that had supported the most by-hand manufacturing workshops. Among the largest industrial towns were Manchester, Leeds, Birmingham, Liverpool, Bristol, London, Sheffield, and Glasgow. The populations of these towns grew extremely rapidly. Manchester, which had only 25,000 people in 1770, had six times as many residents sixty years later, and between 1831 and 1852 the city's population more than doubled to 350,000. Overall, Britain's population rose from 5.7 million in 1750 to 16.6 million in 1850.

By that point, marking the midpoint of the nineteenth century, Britain had unarguably become the globe's industrial and economic powerhouse. And it exerted a profound effect on the economies of many other nations. "Britain's economic predominance was evident at every hand," historian Crane Brinton writes.

It could be seen in the [busy, crowded] London docks, in the thriving financial houses of the city, [in] the mushrooming factory and mining towns [across England and Scotland] and other quarters of the globe as well. British capital [money] and thousands of skilled British workers participated in the construction of French railroads.

As Britain's economy expanded, wealth flowed into the country from all corners of the globe, stimulating the growth of cities and many large public buildings within them.

American trains ran on rails [made] in British mills [and] cotton goods made in [England] clothed a sizable part of the world's population.[8]

Noted scholar of the Industrial Revolution Eric J. Hobsbawm agrees and adds:

An entire world economy was thus built on, or rather around, Britain and this country therefore temporarily rose to a position of global influence and power unparalleled by any state of its relative size before or since, and unlikely to be paralleled by any state in the foreseeable future. There was a moment in the world's history when Britain can be described . . . as its only [large-scale] workshop.[9]

Social Changes

Accompanying the immense growth of industry, industrial towns, and population were significant changes in British lifestyles and social customs and attitudes. According to Stearns, the Industrial Revolution "brought fundamental changes in[to] almost every aspect of human experience—into the habits of thought and the relations between men and women, as well as into systems of production and [economic] exchange."[10]

One important change in attitude was the way people in Britain thought about themselves and their advancing technological society. Britain and other western countries became biased against peoples and nations that still lagged behind. Those who lacked industry were seen as backward or even inferior. This often provided a rationale for Britain to colonize and control these peoples, including the use of force when deemed necessary.

At the same time, much larger and more tangible changes were occurring in the makeup of and interaction between British social classes. The middle class swelled as small business owners, bankers, investors, and managers multiplied and made comfortable livings. The initial effects of industrialization on lower-class workers (laborers, miners, clerks, and so forth) are more controversial. Some evidence suggests that their wages gradually increased over time. But many scholars point out that these increases did not always keep pace with rising prices. This made it very hard for many families to make ends meet. As a result, wives and children often had to find jobs in factories, too, to support desperate families.

Also, working and living conditions in the industrial towns could be harsh. As one observer puts it:

> Excessively long hours, low pay, rigorous discipline, and subhuman working conditions were the most common grievances of early industrial workers. . . . Many workers could not afford decent housing, and if they could afford it they could not always find it. [As a result] fantastic numbers of human beings were jammed [into] overcrowded slums.[11]

Yet no matter what struggles some workers endured, the factories and work sites in which they labored prospered. Overall, thanks to the rise of industry between the mid-1700s and mid-1800s, Britain and its growing global empire thrived and for all intents and purposes appeared invincible. A detailed examination of the major inventions, products, and achievements of the British Industrial Revolution shows more clearly how this extraordinary situation came about.

Chapter Two

TEXTILES LEAD THE WAY

The first manufacturing sector to be transformed by the Industrial Revolution in Britain was textiles. The slow but steady change-over from the home handicraft system to the factory system began in the early to mid-1700s. And it continued for a century, driven in large degree by population increases and the economic markets they created. As the populations of Britain, several other European nations, and European colonies in the Americas grew in the seventeenth and eighteenth centuries, so did demand for cheap cloth to make clothes. The creation of work-saving machines and the factories that housed them was primarily a response to this demand. Later, British textile mills became models copied far and wide as other nations, including the United States, began the process of industrialization.

Cotton Sets the Pace

Coinciding with these events was another of equal importance—the introduction of a versatile new fiber, cotton, to western countries and markets. In Britain and other western countries, wool, which came from sheep, had long been the primary textile product. (Cloth was also made in smaller amounts from flax, which produced linen, and from silk.) The wool spun and woven in British homes and workrooms came from both locally raised sheep and sheep raised in Britain's overseas colonies. Using old-fashioned, hand-operated spindles and looms, British workers turned the wool into cloth for both domestic and foreign consumption. In the early 1700s, woolen goods made up a quarter of Britain's total exports.

In the late 1600s, however, cotton from faraway India began to enter British textile markets. Not long afterward,

Britain's textile mills, which showcased new processes, machines, and power looms, were copied worldwide.

cotton plantations appeared in the West Indies (Caribbean), and Britain began importing cotton fibers from there. By the 1790s the bulk of British cotton came from plantations in the southern United States.

Cotton production involved many steps and was therefore very labor intensive. First, it had to be combed by hand to separate the fibers from the seeds and various impurities; then people had to spin the raw cotton into thread, twist the thread into yarn, and weave it into cloth on a loom. Other steps often applied

were dyeing or bleaching it and thickening the cloth by dunking it in hot water and a claylike compound called fuller's earth and then beating it.

In spite of the large amount of work involved, cotton possesses certain qualities and advantages that caused it to swiftly gain wide popularity. As Manhattan College scholar Jeff Horn explains:

Cotton could play such an important role because of its unique qualities. Thread spun from cotton is both stronger and easier to use than wool, linen, or silk. These properties make it suitable to machine-based production. Both bleaching and dyeing last longer and are more effective on cotton than on other natural fibers. Cotton fabric is also lighter and more washable than these other mainstay textile fabrics. The potential market for cotton, both in Europe and overseas, was therefore greater than for any other textile.[12]

Because of these qualities, demand for cotton rapidly rose. So inventors and other individuals began finding ways to spin, weave, and make clothes from cotton faster and cheaper. Thereafter, cotton became "the pacemaker of industrial change," as Hobsbawm phrases it. The tremendous expansion of cotton manufacture created "a new form of production, the factory."[13] Thanks to increasing mechanization, between 1750 and 1770 British cotton exports increased tenfold. By the 1820s and 1830s cotton products made up half of all Britain's exports. And in 1851 British cotton mills employed more than half a million workers.

Gradual Mechanization

None of this could have happened, of course, without the introduction of new laborsaving devices and machines. It is important to emphasize that these

Who Was the Real Inventor?

In the past two centuries, most books have given credit for the invention of the spinning jenny to English weaver, carpenter, and inventor James Hargreaves (1720–1778). While Hargreaves took credit for the device and was pivotal in marketing it, did he actually conceive it in the first place? A number of modern scholars say no and argue that the real inventor was a more obscure English artisan named Thomas Highs (1718–1803). Supposedly Highs came up with the idea for a machine with multiple spindles and named after his own daughter, whose name was Jenny.

According to this view, Highs could not afford to get patents for his ideas. Also, for reasons unknown he did not finish perfecting the spinning jenny and passed it along to Hargreaves, who made the necessary changes but also took all the credit. It is possible that Highs also invented the water frame. Some evidence suggests that he asked clockmaker John Kay to make a model of this device; but Kay told inventor Richard Arkwright about it, and Arkwright took credit for inventing it. Scholars continue to debate Highs's contributions to the Industrial Revolution.

innovations were mostly very simple in concept and design. And they were introduced slowly, each doing only what was needed in a specific place or process at a given time. Moreover, most of these machines built on or incorporated existing ideas or devices, usually making them more efficient and productive rather than replacing them altogether.

This slow but steady rise in mechanization was crucial to Britain's industrial success. It allowed inventors, business owners, and workers alike to adapt a little at a time to changing technology and work methods. Indeed, "this situation was very fortunate," Hobsbawm says,

for it gave the then pioneer Industrial Revolution an immense, perhaps an essential, push forward.

It put it within the reach of an enterprising, not particularly well-educated or subtle, not particularly wealthy body of businessmen and skilled artisans, operating in a flourishing and expanding economy whose opportunities they could easily seize. In other words, it minimized the basic requirements of skills, of capital [money], of large-scale . . . organization and planning, without which no industrialization can succeed.[14]

The gradual approach to mechanizing Britain's textile industry is well illustrated by the case of the first important work-saving device introduced into that industry. In the early 1730s, a clockmaker named John Kay (1704–1780) created the flying shuttle. In looms up to that time an operator

Clockmaker John Kay created the flying shuttle, an update to previously used wooden shuttles that doubled the speed of the looms.

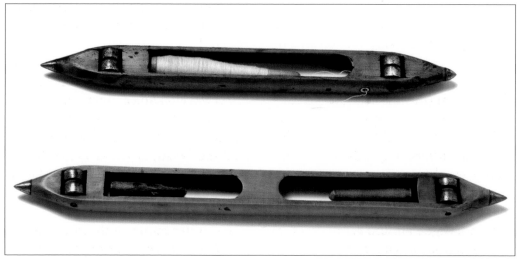

passed a wooden stick called the shuttle back and forth, thereby interweaving the vertical threads (the warp) and the horizontal threads (the weft). In Kay's improved version, the shuttle was mounted on wheels and struck by hammers, which forcefully drove it through the warp. The device doubled the speed of the loom, allowing a weaver to make twice as much cloth in a given amount of time.

The flying shuttle did not make an immediate impact on the textile industry, however. This was because most workers in Lancashire, the region of England in which Kay lived, still clung to tradition. They looked on new machines with suspicion and worried that the new device would make human labor less essential and take away jobs. So an angry mob ransacked Kay's house and he fled to France. There, he tried to market his flying shuttle but encountered similar resistance. It was not until the 1760s that the invention began to see wide use in Britain.

Kay was not the only inventor whose laborsaving ideas took time to catch on with workers. In 1742 Lewis Paul and John Wyatt opened a small textile mill in Birmingham (in west-central England). It featured their roller spinning machine, which consisted of two rollers that turned at different speeds; this action caused wool to spin more uniformly and efficiently. The device aroused little interest, however, and the mill soon went bankrupt. Paul and Wyatt spent the next sixteen years making improvements to their machine and trying it out at different mills.

More Successful New Inventions

Much more successful was the so-called spinning jenny of another Lancashire inventor, James Hargreaves (1720–1778). (He based the device partially on the ideas of another inventor, Thomas Highs.) A large wooden frame with rows of spindles set along each end, it could spin several threads at once, thereby dramatically speeding up the thread-spinning process.

At first, Hargreaves encountered the same kinds of reactions from workers that Kay had, including an attack on his house. However, mill owners in Nottingham (in central England) were impressed and ordered several jennies. The machine caught on there and in nearby towns, and in 1770 Hargreaves obtained a patent for it. By the time of his death eight years later, at least twenty thousand spinning jennies were in use in England.

Meanwhile, in the 1770s a former barber named Richard Arkwright (1732–1792) was enjoying his own success with a device called the water frame. It was based in part on the principles used by Paul and Wyatt, as well as on the ideas of Thomas Highs, whom Arkwright knew. According to Horn:

The water frame, or throstle, was a wooden machine about 32 inches

The First Modern-Style Factory

The first known modern-style factory was a cotton mill built by English inventor Richard Arkwright (1732–1792) in 1771. It was located at Cromford, in Derbyshire (in north-central England). It had many textile machines that were powered by large waterwheels, and it was equipped with arrays of candles to accommodate workers in a night shift. The mill was extremely successful. It rapidly grew in size and soon had thousands of spindles and at least three hundred workers. And by the time of his death, Arkwright was the richest person in Britain outside of the royal family. His mill at Cromford also became a model for other English cotton mills, as well as American and German ones, whose owners copied its layout and methods with positive results. Today, after extensive restorations, the mill is preserved as part of a World Heritage Site.

Richard Arkwright's Cromford Mill, built in 1771 in Cromford, Derbyshire. It was the first modern-style factory, on which all other factories were based. The mill is now a World Heritage Site.

[81cm] high. A wheel was connected to four pairs of rollers to stretch [the] cotton which was then twisted and wound on spindles placed vertically on the machine. Arkwright intended the device to be powered by horses, but water power was swiftly found to be far more economical, giving the machine its name.[15]

Because of these successes and the increased profits they brought to English textile mills, a rash of new textile machines began to appear. Of particular importance, in 1779 inventor Samuel Compton (1753–1827) introduced the spinning mule. The term *mule* (a cross between a horse and a donkey) was a reference to the fact that the device combined elements of two different inventions—the spinning jenny and the water frame. A single spinning mule could accomplish an astounding two hundred to three hundred times as much work as an ordinary hand-driven spinning wheel. Moreover, the mule produced considerably thinner (and therefore more versatile) yet stronger thread.

Another groundbreaking machine was the power loom created by clergyman and inventor Edmund Cartwright (1743–1823). Before him, inventors had mainly tried to increase the amount of work a human spinner or weaver could do using a machine. Cartwright realized that mechanical principles could also be used in conjunction with a separate power source, thereby eliminating the need for human muscle power. "It struck me," he remarked, "that as plain weaving can only be [done in] three movements which were to follow one another in succession, there would be little difficulty in [mechanically] producing them and repeating them."[16] To this end, in the 1780s Cartwright hit upon the idea of installing a series of levers, springs, and gears in a loom. Animal power, and soon afterward steam power, made these parts move.

Several other inventors improved Cartwright's design in the years that followed, and the device slowly but steadily became a staple of the textile industry. By 1813 some 2,400 power looms were in use in Britain; in 1829 there were 55,000; in 1833, 85,000; and in 1850, 224,000.

Two of the many mechanical devices that revolutionized the textile industry after Cartwright's power loom appeared were the cotton gin and the sewing machine. The cotton gin was invented by an American, Eli Whitney, in the 1790s. It separated cotton fiber from the plant's seeds more efficiently, allowing each worker to produce fifty times more cotton than before.

Thereafter, British textile mills were able to import huge amounts of inexpensive cotton from America, which helped fuel the burgeoning Industrial Revolution in Britain. The British textile industry also benefited from practical sewing machines, pioneered in the 1830s, 1840s, and 1850s by American inventors Walter Hunt, Elias Howe, and Isaac M. Singer. Woven cloth could now be stitched together to make clothes much faster and cheaper than before.

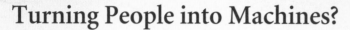

Turning People into Machines?

Although the textile industry created many jobs and much wealth in Britain, some people felt that it also caused many serious social problems. Noted English thinker and social critic Thomas Cooper described some of them in 1823:

The machinery of England is, in many instances, a dreadful curse to that country. . . . The works [factories] usually go night and day. One set of boys and girls go to bed, as another set get up to work. The health, the manners, the morals are all corrupted. They work not for themselves, but for the capitalist [rich factory owner] who employs them. . . . They are machines, as much so as the spindles they superintend [oversee]. The whole system tends to increase the wealth of a few capitalists, at the expense of the health, life, morals, and happiness of the wretches who labor for them.

Quoted in William Dudley, ed., *The Industrial Revolution: Opposing Viewpoints.* San Diego: Greenhaven, 1998, p. 16.

The Factory System

All of these machines that sped up the spinning, weaving, and clothes-making processes had crucial long-term effects on British workers and society. The biggest single change was a transition from home and workshop manufacturing to the factory system. Most people who spun yarn, wove cloth, and made clothes at home could not compete with the new work-saving devices. To keep working and support themselves, a majority of them therefore had to join the labor forces in the new textile mills.

The first major mechanized mill was erected in Cromford, Derbyshire (northwest of Nottingham), in 1771 by Arkwright. Powered by waterwheels, it quickly grew in size and within a few years housed thousands of spindles and some three hundred workers. A mere fifteen years later, 140 similar cotton-spinning mills were in operation in England. And by 1800 the number had grown to about 900.

Not surprisingly, those who benefited most from the new system were the individuals who financed and/or owned the factories. Some were well-to-do investors who saw the potential to make big profits. But others were people of modest means who took a chance and borrowed the money to invest in machines and mills. In 1789, for instance, a middle-class assistant store manager named Robert Owen borrowed one hundred British pounds (the equivalent of several thousand dollars today) and opened a mill in Manchester (in western England). Just twenty years later his investment was worth eighty-four thousand pounds—an enormous fortune worth millions of dollars in an era in which the average British worker made the equivalent of about four hundred dollars per year.

In contrast, for most of the workers the textile factory system was a mixed blessing. On the one hand it did provide steady work for millions of people. On the other hand, working conditions in the mills were more often than not substandard. The prevailing philosophy of most of the

Robert Owen, a middle-class store manager, borrowed several thousand dollars to open his own mill, which later made him millions. Owen also became known for improving the conditions for workers in the mills.

rich industrialists and owners was to keep operating costs down in order to maximize profits. And the salaries and working conditions of the laborers were part of those costs. It was not uncommon, therefore, for owners to require workers to put in sixty- to seventy-hour weeks. Also, the mills were very hot and uncomfortable in the summer, injured workers were fired without compensation, and thousands of children toiled for extremely low wages.

Despite these and many other drawbacks for the workers, the British textile factory system continued to grow and thrive. This was primarily because it was hugely profitable both to the owners and the country itself. Britain experienced "an unprecedented level of economic growth," as Horn puts it. "Britain was the first nation to be able to institute" the "unprecedented economic structure"[17] built on the factory system and the millions of workers it employed. In this way, the emerging textile industry became the model for other industries to follow as the Industrial Revolution continued to transform Britain's economy and society at all levels.

Chapter Three

Coal, Iron, and Steel

Coal, iron, and steel (a very hard form of iron) were among the major and key materials produced during the Industrial Revolution. Iron and steel were leading industrial products, which went into fashioning railroad locomotives and tracks, factory machines, and cannons and other weapons that defended the British Empire.

Coal production was always linked to iron production. This was because coal was used extensively as a fuel for iron making, as well as for steam power and train locomotives, all of which were major components of the widening Industrial Revolution. "If iron was the material basis of the machines that pumped the lifeblood of the Industrial Revolution," Horn writes, "coal provided the power. Although water, wind, and animals all contributed mightily to the energy used in industrialization, without question coal took pride of [first]

place, especially in Britain."[18] Another reason that coal and iron were so closely associated was that coal mines were often located near fields of iron ore.

The importance of iron and coal in expanding British industry is illustrated by the growth in the production of these materials. In 1750 Britain produced only small amounts of iron. But by 1850 it produced more than 150 times more, in total at least half of all the iron made in the world. Also by that date, Britain produced more than 60 million tons of coal, two-thirds of all the coal mined across the globe.

From Charcoal to Coke

These huge increases in coal and iron production occurred in large degree because of the rising need to find alternative and more effective ways of producing energy.

Blaenavon Ironworks in Wales opened in 1788 and became one of the largest ironworks in the world. Three blast furnaces were operated by steam power, and two more were added years later. Blaenavon has become a World Heritage Site because of its major role in the Industrial Revolution.

Both coal and iron were known and used in Britain and other parts of Europe well before the onset of the Industrial Revolution. People had fashioned iron into swords, armor, and other items for centuries. And coal had been used in small ovens and workshops since the 1500s.

But the mining of coal and production of iron had long been small-scale. This was partly because iron was hard to smelt (turn into a liquid state); it required very high temperatures, and making large amounts of it was expensive. Also, the need for coal for fuel was long minimal because people more often used charcoal (made by burning wood) for that purpose. In fact, for centuries the furnaces that smelted iron were powered by charcoal.

Things began to change in the early 1700s, at the same time that simple machines were beginning to transform British agriculture (the precursor to widespread industrialization). Supplies of timber, the main source of charcoal, were rapidly growing short in Britain as people cut down forests at an increasing rate. Coal appeared to be an alternative to charcoal. But burning coal in large quantities had certain drawbacks. First, it generated a lot of smoke and sometimes noxious fumes. Also, ordinary coal did not burn as hot as people would have liked.

A major breakthrough occurred in 1709 when English mill operator Abraham Darby (1678–1717) improved the iron-smelting process by using coke, rather than raw coal, as fuel. Up until that time people smelted iron by placing the iron ore in a big pan and covering it with hot charcoal. They then blew on the charcoal with a bellows operated by hand or by animal power, and the input of air made the charcoal burn hotter. When they substituted coal for charcoal, the coal produced large amounts of smoke. Darby realized that this was because of the water, coal gas, and coal tar trapped in the raw coal. He knew that a purer form of coal—coke—could be made by baking away these excess materials. Coke produced little or no smoke and had the additional advantage of burning hotter than ordinary coal. By using coke in the smelting process, Darby was able to produce iron of much better quality.

New Improvements in Iron Making

Even the iron made by using coke still contained a fair amount of impurities, however, which made it less rigid and strong. These impurities included phosphorus, silica, sulfur, and carbon. A major step in removing these impurities took place in the early 1780s with the invention of iron puddling by English ironmaster Henry Cort (1740–1800). It featured long rods with which a worker stirred the molten iron. As one modern expert explains:

> Bars of [iron] were heated in a furnace by an indirect coal fire. As the bars melted, a "puddler" (also called a rabbler) stirred the liquid. Impurities . . . burned off and the puddled iron formed pasty balls. The puddler would rake these iron balls together to form a large lump weighing a few hundred pounds.[19]

Cort also developed the iron-rolling process. After it had been puddled, the lump of iron was run through a press that squeezed out still more of the silicates. The iron was then squeezed one or two more times by big rollers, shaping it into sheets or bars of the desired size.

Using the new methods introduced by Cort and his technicians, British iron makers were able to turn out iron of very high quality. They were also able to produce the iron much faster than in the past. Fifteen tons of iron could now be made in a mere twelve hours, compared to many days using earlier methods. As a result, the iron industry expanded rapidly in the 1790s and on into the first decades of the nineteenth century.

Shortly before 1750 Britain produced 23,000 tons (20,865t) of iron a year. By the 1850s that figure had grown to an incredible 3.5 million tons (3.2 million t) annually, an increase of 152 times.

Because higher-quality iron could be produced faster and more cheaply, people began to find new uses for it. More and more plows were made of iron instead of wood, for example. All manner of machines, including those in the rising factory system, were composed of iron because of its strength and durability. Iron was used for large-scale construction, including bridges and railroad lines.

One of the leading figures in this iron expansion movement was English indus-

The first blast furnace, created by Abraham Darby. The iron made in these furnaces was stronger and therefore able to be used for larger projects like bridges and railroad lines.

The First All-Iron Bridge

Many bridges were erected in Britain in the late 1700s and early 1800s. One of the more famous, and the first made completely of iron, was the so-called Iron Bridge over the Severn River near the town of Coalbrookdale in western England. Designed by Thomas F. Pritchard and completed in 1779, it is 200 feet (60m) long and 60 feet (18m) high. In the years following its construction, the town of Ironbridge grew up around the bridge, which is still in use. Renovations were made on the structure in 1802, 1972, and again in 1999. The Iron Bridge, one of the first major civil construction works of the Industrial Revolution, is presently part of a World Heritage Site.

The first bridge made completely of iron was the so-called Iron Bridge over the Severn River near the town of Coalbrookdale, in western England.

trialist John Wilkinson (1728–1808), who became known as "iron-mad Jack." He advocated many new uses for iron. He also built an enormous iron-smelting plant at Coalbrookdale, Shropshire (in southwestern England). Wilkinson created a new process that produced better-quality cannons (adding to Britain's military strength), produced iron cylinders for steam engines, turned out iron rotary engines for textile mills, and built iron barges to transport raw materials. He was such a staunch proponent of iron, in fact, that he insisted on being buried in an iron coffin.

In the years following the era of Cort and Wilkinson, more improvements were made in the quality of iron. Perhaps the most important was the introduction of the hot blast furnace. For a long time iron makers had used gusts, or blasts, of air (usually from bellows) to make the charcoal or coke in furnaces hotter. But this air was ordinary room-temperature air. In 1828 Scottish inventor James B. Neilson (1792–1865) successfully used preheated air to stoke iron-smelting furnaces. This both increased the temperature of the coke and reduced the amount of fuel needed in the smelting process. The iron produced this way was strong enough to use in building bigger bridges than in the past, as well as other large structures.

Steel Production

Yet even this high-quality iron was not as strong as steel. Steel is an alloy (mixture) of iron and carbon. Normally, raw iron extracted from iron ore contains small amounts of carbon as one of several impurities. These make the processed iron brittle. This is one reason that iron makers had long tried to remove carbon impurities during the smelting process. However, the presence of a small, specific amount of carbon—between 0.2 and 2 percent—in the mix makes a very strong and durable form of iron—steel.

Steel was made in very small amounts in ancient China, India, Rome, Spain, and Africa. It required heating a piece of iron and then hammering it vigorously and repeatedly. If there was enough carbon present in the iron and the blacksmith managed to achieve the right balance through hammering, he might end up with a little steel. Because this was such a difficult, inexact, and expensive process, large-scale steelmaking did not become practical until the dawn of the Industrial Revolution.

The first major breakthrough occurred in 1740. English inventor Benjamin Huntsman (1704–1776) introduced the crucible process, so named because it utilized small clay containers called crucibles. In his ironworks near Sheffield (in central England), he placed ten to twelve crucibles, each containing a little iron and some other materials, in a hot coke furnace. Then he heated them to extremely high temperatures. This process produced a moderate amount of steel without the need for hammering and in a controlled manner. As a result, British steel production increased considerably—from about 200 tons (181t) a year to some 80,000 tons (72,576t) a year by 1840. This was almost half of all the steel produced in Europe at the time. Another result was that Sheffield became Britain's steel capital and one of the leading industrial cities in the world.

Still, in the mid-nineteenth century steel production accounted for barely a

Henry Bessemer created the Bessemer converter in 1856. The converter was an oval-shaped container that held between 8 and 30 tons (7 and 27t) of iron, and worked by injecting streams of compressed air into the molten iron.

fortieth of the iron industry in Britain. Although plenty of iron was being made, when used for large-scale projects such as bridges and railroad tracks, it was not always strong and reliable enough. Disasters such as bridge collapses occurred too frequently for most people's comfort. A process that could make very large, inexpensive amounts of steel, a more reliable material, was sorely needed.

It was a brilliant English engineer and inventor named Henry Bessemer (1813–1898) who supplied that vital and groundbreaking process. In 1856 Bessemer introduced the so-called Bessemer converter. It was an oval-shaped steel container that held between 8 and 30 tons (7 and 27t) of iron. The converter worked by injecting streams of compressed air into molten iron, thereby accelerating the removal of impurities. When the proportion of carbon in the iron reached the desired level, the process stopped. The process took only twenty minutes, and the result was several tons of steel.

In the 1860s German engineer Carl W. Siemens (1823–1883) and French engineer Pierre-Émile Martin (1824–1915) introduced a different steelmaking method, named the Siemens-Martin process. This open-hearth technique used a large brick chamber that could hold fifty to several hundred tons of iron at a time (depending on the design). The Siemens-Martin process did not replace the Bessemer process; rather, the two coexisted for several decades (until still more effective steelmaking techniques appeared in the mid-twentieth century).

As a result of these advances, steel production in Britain and other indus-

Henry Bessemer—Giant of Industry

Henry Bessemer, one of the giants of Britain's Industrial Revolution, was born in 1813 at Charlton, in Hertfordshire (in southeastern England). The son of an inventor, he showed an early interest in making useful products for society. The younger Bessemer made his first fortune by creating and marketing a powder made from brass. Added to paint, it produced a gold-like effect and became widely popular in decorating fine homes and public buildings. Eventually, Bessemer saw the urgent need for a more economical process to make high-quality steel. A number of bridges made from cast iron had recently collapsed, including the Dee Bridge. The Dee Bridge, near Chester in western England, was a railroad bridge. In May 1847, as a train was passing over it, it gave way, killing five people and injuring many others. Bessemer's answer to the steel shortage was the Bessemer Converter, introduced in 1856. He later patented other inventions, but none was as important and influential as the converter. Bessemer was knighted by Queen Victoria in 1879 and the same year was inducted into the Royal Society (a famous group of scientists and engineers). He died in 1898 in London.

trialized countries increased tenfold between 1865 and 1880. Increasingly, it became possible to use steel, instead of iron, for large-scale structures like bridges. The 6,442-foot Eads Bridge (1,964m), which spans the Mississippi River at St. Louis, was completed in 1874. It used huge amounts of steel, along with lesser amounts of high-quality iron. The first bridge (and first large structure of any kind) built completely from steel was the Forth Bridge in Scotland, finished in 1890. It is 1,710 feet (521m) long.

Coal Production

One far-reaching consequence of the burgeoning iron and steel industry was a parallel growth in coal production. "Coal mining surged to provide the fuel for iron smelting," says Stearns.[20] Yet this was only the tip of the iceberg, so to speak. Coal also powered many textile mills and other factories, steam engines, railroads, and steamships, as well as boilers in many buildings. As a result of swiftly rising demand, the volume of coal production increased enormously throughout the years of Britain's Industrial Revolution. In 1750 the annual output was 4.5 million tons (4 million t); by 1891 it had reached 185 million tons (168 million t), more than forty times as much.

Supplying this tremendous amount of coal required the labor of tens of thousands of workers in hundreds of mines. These were located mainly in northern England (especially in Northumberland, Durham, Lancashire, and Yorkshire) and south Wales. At first, most coal came from pits near the earth's surface. But over time it was necessary to tunnel deeper and deeper. A typical mine consisted of one or more vertical shafts, from which horizontal tunnels, called galleries, branched out, following the veins of coal.

Such work was extremely difficult and often dangerous. One serious obstacle the early miners encountered was a buildup of water in the lower galleries. Sometimes they had to stand in water up to their knees or hips as they worked. This problem was largely alleviated by the introduction of pumps. In 1712 English ironworker and preacher Thomas Newcomen (1664–1729) built a primitive steam-powered pump having a single piston. Other inventors soon improved on the device, and hundreds of such pumps were in use by the mid-1700s.

Another problem was the presence of flammable gases in the mines. Explosions, usually caused by open flames the miners carried to light their way, were common. And they killed or maimed hundreds of workers each year. The danger decreased markedly after 1815, the year that English chemist and inventor Humphry Davy (1778–1829) introduced the safety lamp, which had no exposed flame.

Still other problems, including cramped work spaces and stale air laden with coal dust, persisted, however. As a result, many miners developed serious illnesses. But despite the potential hazards

Expanding British Coal Production

Coal production grew in Britain in direct proportion to the rise of industry. The more steam engines, factories, and railroads created, the more coal was needed to power them. This chart shows expanding British coal production over the course of nearly two centuries.

1700	2.5 million tons (2.3 million metric tons)
1750	4.5 million tons (4 million metric tons)
1800	10 million tons (9.07 million metric tons)
1829	16 million tons (14.5 million metric tons)
1856	65 million tons (59 million metric tons)
1860	70 million tons (63.5 million metric tons)
1891	185 million tons (167.8 metric tons)

involved, there was never a shortage of individuals willing to take the risks. Along with the factory system and iron industry, the coal mining industry provided badly needed jobs for large numbers of British laborers. Thanks to the advent of large-scale industrialization, they could no longer make a living in agriculture. In addition to its many individual machines, the Industrial Revolution had in a sense created a larger, society-wide machine having millions of moving parts—each a British worker doing his or her best to survive.

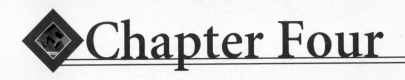

Chapter Four

THE MAINSPRING OF INDUSTRY: STEAM

The machines of the Industrial Revolution needed abundant and relatively inexpensive power to operate. Before the advent of widespread industrialization and during its early years, moving water and animals such as horses provided that power. But soon, steam power was introduced on a large scale. Steam engines most often ran on coal, which was cheaper than oats and the other crops fed to horses, and a single steam engine produced as much work as dozens or even hundreds of horses. This was the origin of the term "horsepower" that became commonly applied to various kinds of modern engines, including those that did not utilize steam.

The effects of steam power on industry in Britain and eventually in other countries was dramatic to say the least. The noted Welsh mill owner, philanthropist, and philosopher Robert Owen, who died in 1858 at the height of Britain's Industrial Revolution, remarked: "The introduction of the steam engine . . . added, in an extraordinary manner, to the powers of human nature. [It has] in half a century multiplied the productive power or the means of creating wealth."[21]

Owen's contemporary, English economist Andrew Ure, went further. Ure correctly foretold how steam power would greatly increase the number of machines in use, thereby transforming not only industry, but also the nature of work and the lives of those who performed and benefited from it:

Steam engines furnish the means . . . of their own multiplication. They create a vast demand for fuel, and while they lend their powerful arms to drain the pits and to raise the coal, they call into employment

One of the first steam engines of the Industrial Revolution. Steam engines ran on coal and produced as much work as hundreds of horses, thus defining the term "horsepower."

multitudes of miners, engineers, ship-builders, and sailors. . . . Steam engines, moreover, by the cheapness and steadiness of their action, fabricate cheap goods, and procure in their exchange a liberal supply of the necessaries and comforts of life. . . . The steam engine is in fact the controller general and mainspring of British industry.[22]

Ure did not exaggerate. By 1850 thousands of steam engines were powering British textile mills, factories, railroad locomotives, and ships, seeming to confirm the popular adage that Britain had become the "world's workshop."

Savery's and Newcomen's Pumps

The concept of steam power was by no means new. Since ancient times inventors had known that when water is heated to its boiling point steam is produced and that the steam expands outward. Then, when the steam cools, it contracts and condenses back into water. In theory, one could force the steam into an airtight container, such as a cylinder. As the steam condenses, a vacuum (space in which no air exists) would form. And a piston (round-shaped rod) attached to the cylinder would move (as a result of normal atmospheric pressure) to fill the vacuum. In turn, the moving piston could be attached to something else to produce some sort of work. The theory was fairly simple and straightforward. But for a long time machinists lacked the expertise to create sufficiently airtight cylinders and the precisely tooled pistons required.

The first practical, though only marginally effective, modern steam engines were built in England in the late 1600s and early 1700s. These were intended

Master of Steam

James Watt, whose contributions to steam power were pivotal to British and world industrialization, was born in 1736 in the Scottish seaport of Greenock. His father was a shipowner. Schooled mostly at home by his mother, Watt displayed a high aptitude for mathematics. In 1758 some professors at Scotland's Glasgow University recognized Watt's talent and allowed him to set up a small workshop on the university's grounds. Four years later, he began to experiment with steam power. Finding that the university had a model of Thomas Newcomen's steam engine, Watt studied it closely and realized that much of the steam's potential was wasted heating the cylinder. Watt decided that it would work better if the steam condensed in a separate chamber. By 1765 he had a working model of his own steam engine. And after a few years, full-scale versions were pumping water out of mines. Eventually Watt teamed up with foundry owner Matthew Boulton, and their company turned out more than a thousand steam engines in the years that followed. Watt died in 1819 at his home in Handsworth (in western England).

mainly to pump water out of coal mines to make the miners' work easier and less dangerous. In 1698 English inventor Thomas Savery (1650–1715) constructed a steam-driven pump that was so primitive that it had no piston or other moving parts. It worked by heating water in an airtight metal boiler. A pipe connected to the boiler projected into the water that needed to be pumped out. When the water in the boiler cooled, condensed, and formed a vacuum, some of the water in the mine was drawn up the pipe and eventually out of the mine shaft. One serious drawback of Savery's device was that it required a lot of heat energy to warm the boiler, much of which was wasted. Also, the vacuum created was only partial, and water could not be raised more than 40 feet (12m).

Thomas Newcomen's steam-driven water pump, which appeared in 1712, was somewhat more complex and considerably more efficient. Ashton describes it:

A great beam of timber, pivoted high above the ground on a solid piece of masonry, was given freedom to swing vertically through the arc of a circle. At one end the beam was connected to a piston, which moved up and down as steam was first injected, and then condensed, in the cylinder. These movements were transmitted to the beam, and so to the pump rods attached to its other end, by movement of which the water was drawn up a pipe in the mine shaft.[23]

Though Newcomen's pump was a definite improvement over Savery's, it, too, had certain drawbacks. Chief among them was that it used a great deal of fuel, making it very energy inefficient. Only about 1 percent of the potential energy contained in the steam was transferred into mechanical energy to move the water. As long as the device was employed at a coal mine, where there was plenty of coal to fuel it, the pump proved useful; but it was too expensive and impractical to use anywhere else.

Watt's Pivotal Advances

Other inventors were sure that steam power had huge potential, however. And in the years that followed they steadily made improvements to Newcomen's engine. In the forefront of this research and development was Scottish instrument maker and inventor James Watt (1736–1819). Although Watt did not invent the steam engine, as is often mistakenly claimed in modern books, he was the first to create affordable versions that could be used for a wide variety of tasks.

After tinkering with Newcomen's steam engine for a while, Watt concluded that having a single cylinder significantly reduced its efficiency. This was because the steam heated the cylinder, after which the cylinder cooled; then the cylinder had to be heated again. It would be much more efficient, he realized, if condensation occurred in a separate

While James Watt (1736-1819) did not invent the steam engine, he created affordable versions that could be used for a wide variety of tasks.

chamber (a condenser), so that the cylinder could maintain its original heat. Watt later recalled how this pivotal idea came to him:

I had gone to take a walk on a fine [Sunday] afternoon. I was thinking on the [Newcomen] engine [and had] gone as far as the Herd's House, when the idea came into my mind that as steam was an elastic [movable and flexible] body, it would rush into a vacuum, and if a communication [connection] was made between the cylinder and [a separate] vessel, it would rush into it and might be there condensed without cooling the cylinder. . . . Two ways of doing this occurred to me, [and] I had not walked further than the golf-house when the whole thing was arranged in my mind.[24]

Watt found that turning his vision into concrete reality was a long, difficult process. First, he had much experimentation to do with cylinders and pistons, which at the time were neither standardized nor precisely engineered and reliable. He also wanted to take out patents on his ideas. These and other aspects of creating his engine were very expensive. And at one point, with his funds exhausted, Watt worked as a surveyor for several years to make ends meet. Eventually, he formed a partnership with a well-to-do backer, Matthew Boulton, who owned an iron foundry in Birmingham. There-after, thanks to Boulton, Watt had both the money to experiment and access to some leading experts in metallurgy. For example, the famous John Wilkinson ("iron-mad Jack") helped Watt to engineer a large, strong cylinder with a tight-fitting piston. By 1776 Watt and Boulton had marketed several of their engines, mostly for use in pumping water out of mines.

Over the course of the next few years, Watt made numerous improvements in his steam engine. One major advance was the sun and planet gear (so named because the rotating gears resembled a planet moving around the sun). Likely the brainchild of one of Watt's and Boulton's engineers, William Murdoch (1754–1839), this ingenious device converted the linear motion of the piston to rotary (circular) motion. Used in thousands of different machines, it became one of the key inventions of the Industrial Revolution.

Another improvement was the double-acting principle, in which steam acted on both sides of the piston. Watt also devised a governor, a device that controlled the speed of the engine by regulating the amount of fuel it used. Watt's contributions to the age of industrialization cannot be overstated. His inventions eliminated the need for water power to make factory machines work. His contributions also led to the development of new machine-building skills. To honor his crucial achievements, scientists named a basic power unit, the watt, after him.

Changing the World

Watt's steam engines were so reliable and popular that by 1824 they could be found in nearly every industrial town in Britain. In addition to water pumps, they powered forges, giant bellows, and other machines in iron foundries; hoisted coal up mine shafts; ran machines that hauled and threshed grain; made train locomotives and large ships move; and powered all manner of textile machines, including large-scale looms. Of these, the steam-powered loom, which appeared in the early 1820s, was among the most revolutionary in its impact on both industry and society.

In his 1823 book *A Compendius History of the Cotton Manufacture*, English economist Richard Guest describes the tremendous advantages of this device:

The steam engine is now applied to the working of the loom, as well as to the preparatory processes [such as cleaning the fibers and spinning them into thread]. A very good hand weaver [will] weave two pieces of [cloth] per week each twenty-four yards long. A steam loom weaver . . . will in the same [amount of] time weave seven similar pieces. A steam loom factory containing two hundred looms, with the assistance of one hundred persons . . . will weave seven hundred pieces per week, of the length and quality before

Machines Have No Souls

In his novel Hard Times, *famed English writer Charles Dickens described a British factory town and its workers, both of which had been transformed by steam power. In the process, he suggested that although steam engines and other machines were useful, there was something undignified and soulless about them.*

Set anywhere, side by side, the work of God and the work of man, and the former . . . will gain in dignity from the comparison. So many hundred hands in this mill, so many hundred horse steam power. It is known, to the force of a single pound weight, what the engine will do, but not all the calculators of the national debt can tell me the capacity for good or evil, for love or hatred, for patriotism or discontent, for the decomposition of virtue into vice, or the reverse, at any single moment in the soul of one of these [human workers].

Charles Dickens, *Hard Times: A Novel.* New York: Harper & Brothers, 1854; originally published as a serial in Dickens's weekly *Household Words*, 1843; repr. New York: W.W. Norton, 1990, p. 56.

described. . . . It may safely be said that the work done in a steam factory containing two hundred looms would, if done by hand weavers, find employment and support for a population of more than two thousand persons.[25]

Another plus was that steam-powered looms could work around the clock, allowing mills to produce enormous quantities of cloth. As a result of the savings that mill owners enjoyed after installing such machines, they were in great demand, and manufacturers could not make them fast enough. By 1835 fully 75 percent of the machines used in Britain's cotton industry operated by steam power.

Not all of the looms and other steam-powered machines installed in the 1820s and thereafter were designed by Watt.

Richard Trevithick (1771–1833) created a high-pressure steam engine that could do more work and was also lighter and more compact. He decided to put his steam engine on wheels, creating the first steam locomotive.

The First Steam-Powered Auto

Some historians of the Industrial Revolution find it curious that no English inventors applied themselves to making a steam-powered locomotive-like vehicle that ran on the ground rather than on tracks—in other words, an automobile. The first such device ever built may have been a self-propelled vehicle created by French military engineer and inventor Nicolas Cugnot (1725–1804) between 1769 and 1771. This steam carriage, for want of a better term, weighed a bit more than 2 tons (1.8t). It had two wheels in the back and one in the front. A large, ungainly steam boiler was propped up just ahead of the front wheel. The carriage did move for short distances. Unfortunately for Cugnot, however, it proved impractical. The boiler had to be relit every ten to fifteen minutes, making travel in the vehicle slower than walking overall. One account claims that the carriage was also unbalanced, making it unstable, and that Cugnot crashed it into a brick wall, although this has not been confirmed. Cugnot's device now rests in France's National Conservatory of Arts and Crafts, in Paris.

French military engineer and inventor Nicolas Cugnot (1725–1804) created the first steam-powered automobile in 1771; however, the car proved impractical because of its slowness and instability.

Several other inventors produced their own steam engines, many of which further improved on his. One of the few shortcomings of Watt's engines was an important one. Namely, they worked on low steam pressure. This was because Watt was convinced that building up too much pressure would cause explosions. Simply put, the steam's low pressure placed limitations on the amount of work an engine could produce.

English mining engineer and inventor Richard Trevithick (1771–1833) managed to overcome these limitations. A leading exponent of what became widely known as "strong steam," he devised a way to make an engine in which the steam was under much higher pressure than in Watt's versions. This enabled Trevithick's engine to do more work than a low-pressure one of the same size. And as a result, the high-pressure version could be built lighter and more compact.

Trevithick's high-pressure engine was reliable and fairly safe. But Watt and other competitors continued to warn about possible dangers. And an unfortunate incident that seemed to support their claims occurred in 1803 in Greenwich (in southern England). Four men were killed when one of Trevithick's steam engines suddenly exploded. The inventor was certain that the accident was caused by the operators' carelessness rather than a design flaw; but the bad publicity forced him to add two safety valves that greatly reduced the chances of similar mishaps.

Another of Trevithick's accomplishments was to mount one of his high-pressure engines on wheels, thereby creating the first steam locomotive (train engine). This made railroads possible and soon led to a revolution in transportation. Coupled with the widespread use of steam in factories and other industrial areas, this ensured steam's preeminent role in remaking the global economy and reshaping everyday life in Britain and elsewhere. As early as the 1780s, some writers were predicting that steam power would change the workings of the civilized world. It later became clear that this was an understatement.

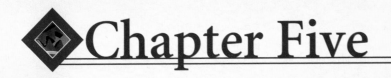

Chapter Five

TRANSPORTATION AND COMMUNICATIONS

Coal, iron, steel, and steam not only made the machine age and mass production of manufactured goods possible, they also transformed Britain's economy and way of life in the 1700s and 1800s by contributing to a transportation revolution of truly enormous proportions. Before the Industrial Revolution, almost all travel and transport of goods was accomplished by walking, riding horses and other animals or on wagons pulled by them, and riding in sailing ships.

Moving from place to place was therefore slow. Ships were faster than the various modes of land travel, to be sure. But their operation was limited to the oceans and those rivers deep enough to accommodate them. Overland transport of coal, iron ore, and other heavy materials necessary to expanding industry remained time-consuming and very expensive. It was impractical for people to carry such materials on their backs. And a single horse could pull little more than half a ton for a short distance before requiring time to rest and eat.

Networks of Canals

One way that business owners and the government improved land transport was to build canals that connected mines and industrial sites to both major rivers and cities. A wave, almost a craze, of canal building transfigured the English countryside. This allowed small ships to carry goods and people long distances much more quickly than before. Also, a barge could be pulled through a canal by horses that walked on a path running along the bank. One horse could pull a waterborne barge loaded with almost thirty tons of cargo.

In 1759, Francis Egerton, Duke of Bridgewater, who owned coal mines in Worsley, proposed building the first canal. It would run from that town a distance of about 10 miles (16km) to Manchester, an industrial city that used his coal. Egerton hired a little-known engineer named James Brindley (1716–1772) to build the waterway. Though lacking a formal education, Brindley had learned from working with an experienced engineer. A skilled, hard-working individual, Brindley finished the Bridgewater Canal in 1761. People came from far and wide to see this first of England's artificial canals, which made him much in demand as a canal engineer.

Brindley's biggest and most famous project was the Grand Trunk Canal, also known as the Trent and Mersey Canal. It consisted of an impressive network of canals of various lengths. Totaling more than 360 miles (580km) in all, they eventually connected to several of England's major western and southern rivers, including the Mersey, Severn, Trent, and Thames. Most of these waterways measured from 20 to 30 feet (6 to 9m) across, wide enough to accommodate narrow barges and boats. Hundreds of

The Trent and Mersey Canal consisted of several different waterways spanning 360 miles. The canal made it possible to transport materials, especially coal, across England for a much smaller cost than land transportation.

The First Passenger Railway

Of the many railroad lines built in England, Scotland, and Wales in the mid- to late 1800s, the first that was a modern-style, intercity, passenger-carrying line was the Liverpool and Manchester Railway. The company was organized in 1823 by businessman and engineer Henry Booth (1788–1869). His goal was to link the bustling port of Liverpool to the growing mill city of Manchester, both in northwestern England. The engineers on the project were George Rennie and John Rennie.

When completed in 1830, the line was 35 miles (56km) long and featured sixty-four bridges, then seen as an impressive overall feat of engineering and construction. The initial locomotive that pulled the first train in September 1830 was the famous *Rocket*, built by Robert Stephenson. In a twist of fate, the opening-day ceremonies were tarnished by a tragic accident. A prominent member of Parliament stepped onto the tracks at the wrong moment and the *Rocket* ran him over, killing him.

Liverpool and Manchester Railway coach from the early 1800s. The railway was the first modern intercity passenger line.

small bridges were erected to carry foot, horse, wagon, and carriage traffic across the canals.

When the Grand Trunk's Thames section opened in 1790, it allowed transport of coal from the mines of western England to London for a fraction of what it had cost before. And coal was only one of many products carried on this and other English canals built in England between 1760 and 1830. Their total length was almost 4,000 miles (6,400km). About the significant benefits of these waterways, Ashton writes:

> The cost of bulky or heavy commodities such as coal, iron, timber, stone, salt, and clay was greatly reduced. Agricultural regions which had been remote from the market were brought within the widening circle of exchange. The fear of local famine, of both food and fuel, was removed. [Also] the incomes paid out to those who dug the canals, when spent, resulted in a raising of level of employment generally. . . . Perhaps the most important result [of the canal building] was that it trained up a new race of engineers, equipped to meet the calls which the age of the railways was to make on their skill, endurance, and capacity for disciplined effort.[26]

From Wagonways to Railways

Even more successful in making land travel cheaper and more efficient were railroads. Britain pioneered the first railroad locomotives and long lines of rails (tracks) connecting cities and/or industrial sites. Like so many other features of the Industrial Revolution, railroad lines and networks built upon existing facilities and systems. Beginning in the early 1600s, many miles of wagonways were laid in several parts of England. These were wooden rails on which horse-drawn wagons moved, carrying coal and other materials from mines to rivers and towns. The wagons' motion was smoother and faster on these rails (which cradled the wagon wheels) than on muddy, dusty, rock-strewn roads.

In 1768 the Coalrockdale ironworks took a step toward true railroads by laying iron plates over the wooden rails it had been using for transport. And a few years later both the wooden rails and iron plates were replaced by smooth-edged iron rails. Each rail was about 3 feet (1m) long and rested on stone blocks laid on the ground at intervals. Eventually, as more sophisticated railroads spread across the countryside, longer iron rails were laid, and in 1857 steel ones began to replace them. Thereafter, a rail gauge (the distance between the two rails) of 4 feet 8½ inches (1.435m) became standard in Britain and most other countries.

As for the locomotives (train engines) that traveled on these rails, the first workable steam-powered version was built by Trevithick. Among his many experiments with high-pressure steam engines was one in which he mounted an engine on wheels and placed it on an existing metal-covered

The Impact of Railroads

Two experts on the Industrial Revolution here concisely summarize the overall advantages and impact of the first railroads on Britain's industry and economy.

The speed and reliability of railroads (which unlike canals or rivers did not freeze over in the wintertime) enabled [industrial] producers to dramatically increase the volume and speed with which goods were shipped. [In addition] thanks to the railroad, postal rates fell dramatically in industrial countries during the mid-nineteenth century. This development was accompanied by the explosive growth of the telegraph system. Together, these two developments enabled the coordination of efficient, safe shipments of goods by the railroads.

Peter N. Stearns and John H. Hinshaw, *The ABC-CLIO World History Companion to the Industrial Revolution.* Santa Barbara, CA: ABC-CLIO, 1996, pp. 207.

---

wagonway. This primitive but impressive locomotive hauled 10 tons (9.1t) of iron, seventy men, and five wagons a distance of 9 miles (14.5km) from a rural iron foundry to the Welsh town of Merthyr Tydfil in February 1804.

Other inventors experimented with steam locomotives in the years that followed. Notable was Matthew Murray (1765–1826). In 1812 his locomotive, dubbed the *Salamanca,* replaced horse-drawn wagons on the Middleton Railway, which ran from some coal pits to the industrial town of Leeds.

Most famous of all was the *Rocket,* a steam locomotive created by Robert Stephenson (1803–1859), son of railroad pioneer George Stephenson (1781–1848). It made its debut in 1829. In a widely publicized contest of steam locomotives, it won first prize and the following year became the first train engine to operate on the Liverpool and Manchester Railway; this was the world's first modern-style intercity passenger railroad line.

After that, Britain's railroad system expanded at a phenomenal rate. By 1838 its various railways lines had a combined length of 500 miles (805km); by 1850, 6,600 miles (10,626km); and by 1870, 15,500 miles (24,955km). These trains did more than revolutionize shipping and travel by carrying enormous amounts of raw materials and manufactured products and large numbers of passengers. They also helped Britain's economy by expanding employment. Tens of thousands of workers were needed to build the trains and tracks, lay new railway lines (including building bridges and tunnels for the trains), maintain the lines, and staff the trains and railroad stations and offices.

Early Steamboats

At the same time that iron rails were spreading across Britain's landscape, enterprising individuals were beginning to apply steam power to boats. One of the first attempts to accomplish this task was made in the early 1700s by Newcomen, whose steam-powered water pump made mining easier and safer. Unfortunately, his engine lacked the power to move a large boat. Several French inventors also tried but failed to create a practical steamboat in that century.

The first practical steamboat was the *Charlotte Dundas*, launched in 1802 by Scottish engineer William Symington (1764–1831). It successfully towed two 70-ton (63.5t) barges 19 miles (30km) along the Forth and Clyde Canal (in the Scottish lowlands). American inventor Robert Fulton (1765–1815) visited Scotland and saw the boat in action. And the following year he built his first steamboat and tested it in France. Other famous early steamboats built in Britain included the *Comet* (1812) and the *James Watt* (1820).

These small ships paved the way for large-scale steamboat production in both Britain and the United States. By 1827 Britain had 232 of these vessels; twenty years later that number had increased to 924. Most of these boats used paddlewheels (rotating blades that pushed on the water, propelling the boat forward). The screw (or propeller), also powered

The SS Sirius *was the first steamship to cross the Atlantic. It left Ireland on April 3, 1838, and arrived in New York eighteen days later.*

A Telegraph Line Celebrated in Song

The laying of the first permanent, successful transatlantic cable in 1866 inspired several popular songs, including one with these words:

Done! The angry sea consents,
The nations stand no more apart;
With clasped hands the continents
Feel throbbings of each other's heart.

Speed! Speed the cable! Let it run
A loving girdle round the earth,

Till all the nations 'neath the sun
Shall be as brothers of one hearth.

As brothers pledging, hand in hand,
One freedom for the world abroad,
One commerce over every land,
One language, and one God.

Quoted in J. Munro, *Heroes of the Telegraph*, part 2, FullBooks.com. www.fullbooks.com/Heroes-of-the-Telegraph2.html.

by the steam engine, began to see practical use in the late 1830s and 1840s and helped to make large seagoing steamships practical. The first steamship to cross the Atlantic nonstop was the *Sirius*. "She left Ireland on 3 April 1838," one modern observer writes,

> encountering stormy weather, snow, and an attempted mutiny during the voyage, but arriving safely in New York in 18 days. . . . Her triumph was eclipsed the next day when [the large steamship the] *Great Western* arrived in New York, breaking her record by three days. The same indignity would happen on the return journey: *Sirius* set an eastbound record of 18 days, broken by *Great Western* in 15 days.[27]

Advances in Communications

These voyages by steam-powered ships cut the time needed to cross the Atlantic (and other oceans) in half, in the process increasing the speed of communications between continents. But even more dramatic advances in communications soon followed. They were possible because of recent scientific breakthroughs in harnessing one of nature's most potent powers—electricity.

In the 1790s Italian researcher Alessandro Volta (1745–1827) created the voltaic pile. A forerunner of the electric battery, it produced a weak but steady stream of electricity. A much bigger milestone occurred in 1831 when English chemist Michael Faraday (1791–1867) discovered that a rotating magnet could generate electricity in a metal wire. He also built an electric motor. A

Belgian, Zénobe Gramme (1826–1901), carried this a step further by constructing a device that produced a steady, reliable electric current.

On the one hand, these developments led to attempts to replace steam with electricity in many factories. On the other hand, they led to the introduction of the telegraph, a device for sending messages over long distances, in the late 1830s. Among the pioneers of the new field of telegraphy were British scientists William Cooke (1806–1901) and Charles Wheatstone (1802–1875). An electrical current moving through a wire activated an electrical field, causing a needle to indicate a letter printed on a dial.

The impact of the telegraph on both industry, society, and even warfare in the mid- to late 1800s was huge. Both railroads and shipping lines used the new invention to improve their planning and schedules; business deals and transactions became quicker and more profitable; and armies, which were starting to employ advanced weapons produced by industry, could more effectively carry out battlefield strategies and maneuvers.

Laying of the transatlantic telegraph cable in 1866 led to faster communication between Britain and North America. Here, cable is passed to a ship that will then load it aboard the Great Eastern—*the ship responsible for laying the telegraph across the Atlantic Ocean.*

Also, the world became smaller in the sense that people could communicate over vast distances in mere seconds. In 1851 a telegraph cable was laid in the English Channel, linking England with the rest of Europe. And in 1866 the first permanent, successful transatlantic cable, sponsored by a joint British-American company, went into operation, connecting Britain to North America. The first message it carried came from England, quoting an article printed the same day in the *Times* of London. "It is a great work," it said in part, "a glory to our age and nation, and the men who have achieved it deserve to be honored among the benefactors of their race."[28] To the British people, these words fittingly reflected their pride in their nation's industrial and technological achievements, which at that moment were the envy of the world.

Together, the transportation and communications revolutions in a sense broadened the scope of the Industrial Revolution. Already established components of industrialization (coal, iron, and steam) were forced to expand and modify to accommodate newer ones. Stearns explains:

> [Steamships] and railroads, plus faster communication via the newly invented telegraph, truly revolutionized the conveyance of goods, people, and information. More bulk could be transported over longer distances at greater speed than ever before. [In turn, this] generated additional change. . . . Coal and iron production had to expand simply to meet the demand generated by railroad construction and operation. The Industrial Revolution was beginning to feed itself, sprouting new branches to deal with opportunities presented by prior developments.[29]

Chapter Six

THE IMPACT OF
INDUSTRIALIZATION

The onset of the Industrial Revolution had an enormous impact on Britain and later on other nations as they either became industrialized or provided raw materials to feed the ever-growing British industrial giant. In addition to altering the nature of industry, manufacturing, and work, industrialization had far-reaching effects on British society and Britain's position in world affairs. These included the emergence of a new industrial working class in Britain, workers' protests over substandard working conditions in factories, changing political views and laws to cope with industrialization, the rapid growth of cities, increasing environmental problems caused by industry, and exploitation of British colonies and foreign lands to support British industry. As a result of all of these factors, by the late 1800s Britain was a very different place than it had been in the early 1700s.

Business Owners and Workers

Among the more significant developments that occurred during the era of industrialization was the rise of two new socioeconomic groups in Britain. The smaller one, made up of a new class of wealthy factory and business owners, emerged in the early 1800s. Because they invested and made large amounts of money—in economic terms "capital"—they are often called capitalists. Their overall success made Britain wealthier and more influential; so the government tended to pass laws that supported their interests, often at the expense of the people who worked for them.

These industrial workers made up the larger of the two new socioeconomic groups. It formed as millions of people moved from rural areas to the fast-growing cities and took jobs in the new factories. Some early factory workers made decent wages, particularly those with special skills. But over time the vast majority of workers had to cope with low pay, as factory owners, seeking to maximize their profits, cut costs any way they could. "Many employers," Stearns points out, were

> desperate for workers but desperate also to keep costs down. [This] was the inspiration for hiring groups of orphans from London and other large towns, who were shipped in droves to the factory centers. . . . Extensive use of child and female labor . . . specifically because of the low wages [they made] reflected the pressures of early industrial life.[30]

Moreover, the early workers had many other problems to deal with besides low wages. They received no sick pay or old-age pensions, for example. In fact numerous employers docked a person's pay if he or she did not show up for work, sick or

It was not uncommon for children to be working in the cotton mills, which were often dangerous. By the end of the nineteenth century, child labor had been banned.

not. Also, the workers put in long hours, often up to sixteen hours a day, with only Sundays off. In addition, working conditions in factories were frequently dangerous and uncomfortable.

Cotton mills were a prominent example. Because cotton threads broke less easily in hot, humid air, employers turned up the heat in their mills. In 1824 a British journalist told how cotton spinners endured temperatures of up to 84°F (29°C). "These poor creatures have no cool room to retreat to," he wrote, "not a moment to wipe off the sweat, and not a breath of [fresh] air [for hours at a time]. The door of the [mill] is locked, except half an hour [a day, and] the workpeople are not allowed to send for water to drink."[31]

The workers' living conditions were often little better. Life in the early industrial towns was typically grim, with cramped housing, filthy streets, and frequent outbreaks of cholera and other contagious diseases. As a result, death rates among the workers rose in the early 1800s. Also, schools were few. As late as the 1840s, a third of the men and fully half of the women in England were illiterate. Living conditions in the industrial centers improved somewhat in that decade as the government began to tackle some of these problems. But major improvements did not occur until the last years of the century.

Impact on the Environment

Workers' housing, as well as other sectors of the cities and countryside, were adversely affected by a general environmental decline. During the first century of the Industrial Revolution, thousands of new factories belched soot-laden smoke into the air, creating smog and other kinds of air pollution. Factories routinely dumped unprocessed human and animal wastes into rivers and lakes. Local waterways also became receptacles for toxic industrial wastes, including chemicals dangerous to humans.

In addition, the early railroads cut across farmlands, polluting the air and frequently injuring livestock; dams built for water power created lakes that drowned former farmlands; unsightly slag heaps (piles of mining wastes) multiplied in many sections of the countryside; and the building of canals, railroads, bridges, and factories, as well as polluting, destroyed animal habitats. Many species of fish disappeared from the Thames and other rivers, for instance.

While some of these developments were detrimental to the health of humans and animals, others marred the country's natural beauty. Britain's legislature, Parliament, began to remedy the situation in the mid- to late 1800s, including installing a large sewer system in London and enacting various regulations that limited dumping wastes into the environment. Overall, however, such regulations came a few at a time and were often ignored by industrial polluters. It was not until the twentieth century that major strides were made in improving Britain's environment.

The British Morally Superior?

A number of nineteenth-century British writers concluded that their country's industrial success and preeminence was not an accident; rather, it stemmed largely from certain qualities inherent in the British people, including patriotism, ingenuity, and moral and racial superiority. One of these writers, Samuel Smiles, wrote in 1859:

[B]ritain's] national progress is the sum of individual industry, energy, and [moral] uprightness. . . . The highest patriotism and philanthropy [chari-table giving] consist [in] helping and stimulating men to elevate and improve themselves by their own free and independent action as individuals. . . . One of the most strongly marked features of the English people is their indomitable spirit of industry. [It] is this spirit, displayed by the [common people] of England, which has laid the foundations and built up the industrial greatness of empire at home and in the colonies.

Samuel Smiles, *Self-Help; with Illustrations of Character and Conduct.* London: John Murray, 1859, pp. 2, 8, 21.

Changing Political and Social Ideas

One of the main reasons that such reforms were slow in coming was a general reluctance on the part of British legislators to interfere with big business. The initial reaction of most politicians, economists, and thinkers was that a certain amount of suffering is a natural part of the human condition. Thus, it was unfortunate but inevitable that progress would have some negative consequences, and these must be accepted. One contemporary observer put it this way:

"Suffering and evil are nature's admonitions [slaps on the wrist]; they cannot be got rid of. And the impatient attempts of benevolence [good intentions] to banish them from the world by legislation . . . have always been more productive than good.[32]

Not surprisingly, leaders of industry embraced this concept and used it to rationalize (excuse) their ongoing exploitation of the workers. "It was consoling to the rich," a modern scholar writes, "to be told in effect that the poor deserved to be poor because . . . whatever was, was right, or at any rate ordained by nature."[33] It was not the fault of factory owners and politicians, the reasoning went, that the lower classes had large families they could barely afford to feed. At least the factories provided them with jobs, however strenuous and low-paying these might be.

What those who argued this way did not foresee was that, as the Industrial Revolution unfolded, certain factors would come into play to relieve the miseries of the working class. These included an economic expansion so huge that employers could raise workers' wages and still make a large profit; scientific advances that allowed agriculture to sustain a larger population and curb hunger; widespread use of contraceptives, allowing workers to have smaller families; and immigration of many workers to Europe, the Americas, and elsewhere, helping to slow Britain's population growth.

In addition to these developments, as the nineteenth century progressed, more humane attitudes set in among

As the Industrial Revolution unfolded, some philosophers and politicians proposed workers be treated more fairly with wages and accessibility to better housing. Row houses were often built near factories for the working class of the town.

the British elite. Some philosophers and politicians began to propose that society be reorganized to make industry, labor relations, and people's lives more fair, equitable, and happy. One was English political economist John Stuart Mill (1806–1873). "By what means, then, is poverty to be contended against?" he asked in one of his widely read books. "How is the evil of low wages to be remedied? . . . Is the problem incapable of solution?"[34] Mill's answer to this last question was "no." His suggested remedies included providing more education for the masses, allowing workers to form trade unions, paying workers higher wages and in some cases allowing them to share in company profits, enacting legislation to protect child laborers and improve workers' living conditions, and granting women the same political rights as men.

Not all of these solutions were implemented fully in the 1800s. But by the end of that century most child labor had been banned and new regulations significantly reduced the length of the workday. Also, the government established many new secondary schools and colleges, greatly expanding educational opportunities for the lower and middle classes. In addition, some factory owners followed the lead of wealthy businessman Robert Owen. Well before Parliament began enacting reforms, he voluntarily improved the lot of his workers; he reduced their hours, raised their wages, and provided schooling for all children in the working families.

Workers' Reactions and Protests

It is important to emphasize that the factory workers and other laborers of the Industrial Revolution in Britain did not always sit back and wait for reform imposed from above. Some workers openly protested what they saw as unfair treatment by employers. In fact, in the early years of industrialization a number of workers actually tried to stop it from going forward by vandalizing and destroying machines and factories.

Most of the violence occurred between 1800 and 1820. It was inspired by anger over the loss of hand manufacturing jobs to the rising factory system and what workers viewed as poor treatment of them by the factory owners. These extremists became known as Luddites. The term derived from "Ned Ludd," a mythical individual who supposedly led the movement and penned warnings sent to factory owners. Typical was the following message delivered to the owner of a textile mill in 1812:

Information has just been given [that] you are a holder of those detestable shearing frames [textile machines], and I was desired by my men to write to you, and give you fair warning to pull them down. . . . If they are not taken down by the end of next week, I shall [send] at least 300 men to destroy them [and] we will increase your misfortunes by burning your buildings down to ashes, and if you have the impudence to fire at any of my men, they have orders to murder you. . . . Signed by the General of the Army of Redressers. Ned Ludd.[35]

Though audacious and headline-grabbing, these periodic threats and attacks had almost no effect on Britain's massive industrial institutions. So eventually the Luddites became discouraged and gave up. However, other workers took the route of peaceful protests, such as public calls for better wages and working conditions. They also formed various labor organizations and brotherhoods of workers. One goal was to stage strikes in hopes of pressuring factory owners and big business owners to

In the early years of the Industrial Revolution, some workers were angered by the loss of hand manufacturing jobs to the factory system. These men were known as Luddites and rebelled by vandalizing machines and threatening factory owners with violence.

A Luddite Oath of Loyalty

The Luddites' success in disrupting factories and industry depended in large degree on secrecy and the loyalty of the organization's members. For that reason, they often recited oaths, including this one, promising not to betray one another.

I, [the person's name], of my own free will [do] hereby promise and swear that I will never reveal any of the names of any one of this secret committee, under the penalty of being sent out of this world [i.e., killed] by the first brother [fellow Luddite] that may meet me. I furthermore do swear that I will [be] sober and faithful in all my dealings with all my brothers, and if ever I decline them, my name [is] to be blotted out from the list of society and never to be remembered . . . so help me God to keep this our oath inviolate [intact].

Quoted in James L. Outman et al., eds., *Industrial Revolution: Primary Sources.* Detroit: Thomson Gale, 2003, p. 67.

address the workers' grievances. More often than not, though, these efforts were unsuccessful. This was mainly because the government, anxious to support and appease big business, passed laws making many organized labor activities illegal and sent in police to break up strikes and protests. In addition, employers frequently fired strikers or evicted them from their homes. (The employers often owned the housing surrounding the factories.) For these reasons, major gains by organized labor did not begin to occur until the late 1800s.

Global Developments

Meanwhile, Britain's Industrial Revolution was also having a powerful effect on other countries, as well as on Britain's pivotal place in the world. First, in the early to mid-1800s large-scale industrialization began to spread to the United States and large sections of Europe (especially France, Belgium, and Germany). And by 1900 Russia, Japan, Sweden, and several other nations were rapidly industrializing. Moreover, "even parts of the world that did not industrialize," scholar Laura L. Frader points out,

were touched by the power of new inventions, machines, and manufacturing processes and by the products that the wheels of industry churned out. . . . The captains of industry produced goods in order to sell, trade, or barter them, and their commercial activities circled the globe.[36]

Russia's Great New Railroad

One important way that Britain's industrial revolution impacted the world was to stimulate large-scale industrialization in other nations. One of the first to follow the British lead was Russia. In 1892 the Russians began building the Trans-Siberian Railway, which eventually linked Moscow to Vladivostok, on the other side of the Asian continent. In 1900 a British diplomat witnessed the railway's ongoing construction and commented:

I t is indeed not too much to say that the completion of this gigantic thoroughfare [transportation route] will, commercially and otherwise, be one of the greatest events of the opening years of the new century. Dealing with a vast expanse of territory exceeding in area the whole of Europe, and some 40 times the size of the British Isles, it . . . will give the desired impetus to colonization and development, and by making the whole country a vast transit route between east and west, open it out to the whole world.

Quoted in Laura L. Frader, *The Industrial Revolution: A History in Documents.* New York: Oxford University Press, 2006, pp. 108.

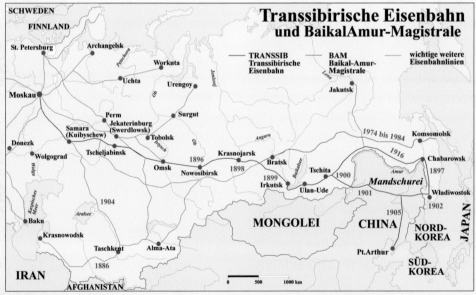

Russia was among the first countries to follow the lead in large-scale industrialization behind Britain. In 1892 the Russians began building the Trans-Siberian Railway, which eventually linked Moscow to Vladivostok.

Also, the Industrial Revolution promoted the growth of global empires, of which Britain's was by far the largest. British industrialists needed to maintain a continuous supply of raw materials and markets in which they could sell their finished goods. To these ends, they exploited nonindustrialized (or undeveloped) countries and regions. In some cases Britain seized control of a region and made it a colony. But more often it made deals with foreign peoples to exchange their native raw materials for British manufactured goods. These peoples then became heavily dependent economically on trade with Britain and its empire and informally became part of that domain.

To maintain such relationships, the British enacted treaties, which not surprisingly always favored themselves. But when necessary they resorted to force. Britain's navy was the world's largest, and its armies were highly organized and well trained. Through trade, negotiation, and occasional armed force, therefore, the British became involved in Australia, Singapore, China, India, Egypt, South Africa, and numerous other places. It was in this period that someone coined the now famous phrase "The sun never sets on the British Empire." Horn aptly sums up the strong connection between industrialization and the global domination achieved by Britain and other western industrialized powers:

The Industrial Revolution facilitated the development of Western military superiority and the new, improved means of transportation tied the globe together in a far more concrete manner, allowing the exploitation of vast new areas. At minimal cost, [the British and other] Europeans and their descendants came to enjoy an unprecedented degree of world domination as a result of the Industrial Revolution.[37]

Chapter Seven

A Host of Engineering Marvels

In addition to helping Britain's global empire to expand, that nation's Industrial Revolution produced a number of imposing monuments and other civil engineering projects that trumpeted British progress to the world. One noted historian said: "Among the new [British] industries to which the eighteenth century gave rise, perhaps the most important was engineering."[38] Industrial Britain's host of engineering marvels included canals, tunnels, huge metal ships, and other large-scale constructions, many of which survived well into the twentieth century.

Besides a few large cathedrals and palaces, very few big engineering projects had been attempted in England or other parts of Europe in the centuries leading up to the Industrial Revolution. In part this was because few people had the talent and skill to create such structures. And most of them worked for the military. They erected forts and other defenses and designed and built warships.

In the late 1600s, with tensions among European nations rising, France, England, and some other countries began to rely more heavily on these military engineers. At the same time, however, some national leaders recognized the need for creating new civil engineering projects such as roads and bridges. So, many of the military engineers began applying themselves to such civil projects.

To train young engineers, different countries took different approaches. France, for example, pioneered the first engineering schools. L'Ecole Royale des Ponts et Chaussées, established in Paris in 1747, was the first such institution in the world. In England, by contrast, engineers trained in the apprentice system. That is, a person who had established himself as a professional in the field took in young helpers and taught them what he knew.

Before the mid-1700s most of the projects these English masters and apprentices worked on were windmills and waterwheels. Both used natural forces to perform work, such as making large millstones move. Because the term "engineer" had not yet been coined, these skilled individuals were most often called millwrights.

The success of the Industrial Revolution was due largely to the engineers of its time, including George Stephenson (1781–1848), who built the first steam locomotive and designed the first commercially successful railway.

Over time the apprentice system began to produce more specialized engineers. Some, like James Watt, became inventors who built specific machines and devices such as steam engines. Others devoted themselves to building large-scale civil projects, including canals, bridges, tunnels, and huge buildings. And they passed their knowledge on to their assistants. According to one observer:

Apprentices had the work ethic instilled in them by long hours of labor. [Work from] 6 A.M. to 5 P.M., followed by technical study until 10 P.M., was not uncommon. In this respect, apprentices imitated great engineers like [Isambard K.] Brunel, who would frequently work for 36 hours without a break. Possession of these abilities fostered belief in the engineer as a "practical man," able to harness a wide variety of skills to complete innovative projects. The results were some of the greatest achievements [and symbols] of the Industrial Revolution.[39]

The Great Tunnels

Of these engineering achievements, the earliest notable examples were canals and tunnels. The networks of canals created by James Brindley and other noteworthy engineers were not only highly practical but also seen as wonders of planning and construction. The same can be said for the many tunnels that engineers and their crews carved into hillsides. Some tunnels helped the coal mining industry, while others were built by the railroads so that trains did not have to travel all the way around hills and mountains. The earliest of these tunnels were relatively small, but they laid the groundwork for much larger ones, which became true engineering marvels.

Among the greatest of these underground throughways was the Thames Tunnel, built between 1825 and 1843. The first tunnel ever constructed beneath a river, it linked the opposing banks of the mighty Thames River in London. The engineers were two of the finest that Britain ever produced—Marc I. Brunel (1769–1849) and his son Isambard K. Brunel (1806–1859). The work was extremely arduous. This was partly because the tunnel lay at a depth of 75 feet (23m) below the riverbed. And some of the workers, along with the younger Brunel himself, became ill from sewage-laden water seeping down from the river. But when completed, the tunnel awed all who beheld it. It measured 35 feet (11m) wide, 20 feet (6m) high, and the then amazing length of 1,300 feet (396m).

Another famous and somewhat longer tunnel, the Tower Subway, also in London, was built in a single year and opened in 1870. One reason for the swiftness of construction was that the engineer, James H. Greathead (1844–1896), had access to more advanced tunneling tools and technology than the Brunels had three decades before. The completed Tower Subway was 1,350 feet (410m) long and

Britain's Triumph

In its May 3, 1851, edition, the English publication Economist *marked the opening of the Great Exhibition with this expression of pride in the ongoing British economic and imperial achievement:*

[B]ritain is] the mightiest empire of the globe—the empire in which industry is the most successfully cultivated, and in which its triumphs have been the greatest. . . . The contrast and the change we have noticed, [including] the present devotion to peace, and the former appliance to war, telling of a future still more peaceful than the present; [and] a future when [the] skill of the laborer shall be held in still higher honor . . . are convincing proofs of the moral improvement already made; and they give us irresistible assurances that a yet higher destiny awaits our successors even on earth.

Quoted in Philip A.M. Taylor, ed., *The Industrial Revolution in Britain: Triumph or Disaster?* Boston: D.C. Heath, 1970, p. xi.

at first featured a small subway train that carried passengers. Later, the train and tracks were removed and commuters walked through the tunnel. Today, it is still in good condition and carries water pipes and TV cables.

Brunel's *Great Eastern*

Although the Thames Tunnel was widely seen as the achievement of a lifetime, it was only one of many large-scale projects tackled by the great Isambard Brunel. He also designed bridges and railways. These included the 700-foot Clifton Suspension Bridge (213m) in Bristol and the Great Western Railway that linked London to southwest England.

But Brunel's greatest engineering accomplishments were his giant steamships. The first, which created a sensation with the press and public, was the *Great Eastern*. Measuring 236 feet (72m) in length, it was made of wood and ran by a combination of steam and sail power. When launched in 1837, it cut the average trip from Britain to New York and back from two months to less than one. In 1843 Brunel made history again with his *Great Britain*. At a length of 322 feet (98m), it was the world's first large steamship with an iron hull.

Brunel created a trend toward bigger and bigger vessels. He strongly believed (correctly as it turned out) that ships of the future, whether for passengers, freight, or war, would be extremely large. "Size in a ship is an element of speed," he said, "and of strength and of safety, and of great relative economy."[40]

As a result, Brunel set out to surpass himself once more by creating the world's largest ship, which he named the *Great Eastern*. "I have never embarked on any one thing," he stated, "to which I have entirely devoted myself, and to which I have devoted so much time, thought, and labor."[41] Launched in 1858, the *Great Eastern* was an incredible 690 feet (211m) long, 82 feet (25m) wide, had five steam-powered engines, and carried 4,000

Engineer Isambard Brunel (far left) in front of his Great Eastern. *With five steam-powered engines and carrying 4,000 passengers and 418 crew, the* Great Eastern *was the world's largest steamship.*

Shipbuilding Dangers and Accidents

British historian Deborah Cadbury here describes some of the mishaps that occurred during the building of Brunel's mighty steamship, the Great Eastern. *Though tragic, such incidents were typical of large-scale industrial projects in the nineteenth century.*

Working in the dark, confined space of the [ship's] double hull, it did not do to lose concentration, even after a 12-hour shift. One moment of carelessness could be paid for with a hand, or an arm, or a life. Accidents were commonplace. It was all too easy to miss a step and, falling from a height, involve another man in disaster in the overcrowded conditions. One worker, making bolts, got his hands tangled in the machinery and torn completely from their sockets at the wrist. In his case, amputation of both arms was the only solution. Another man . . . was bent over examining the machinery when [a steam] hammer came down, flattening his head. Children were particularly vulnerable. . . . One unfortunate child fell from a height and was impaled on an upright iron bar.

Quoted in Deborah Cadbury, *Dreams of Iron and Steel: Seven Wonders of the Nineteenth Century.* New York: Fourth Estate, 2004, p. 9.

passengers and 418 crew. "Nothing like this had ever been seen before," historian Deborah Cadbury writes. It was at the time "the largest man-made object ever built and, for many, a symbol of the greatness of the British Empire"[42] and its industrial might. All Englishmen were indeed proud of Brunel's achievement, as reflected in glowing terms in a major English newspaper: "Owing to the great beauty of her lines, she cuts the waves with the ease and quietness of a knife, her motion being just sufficient to let you know that you have no dead weight beneath your feet, but a ship that skims the waters like a thing of life."[43]

Overcoming the "Great Stink"

While large-scale projects like canals and giant ships expanded Britain's economy and spread the products of the Industrial Revolution far and wide, other engineering works sought to improve people's lives. Among the most notable examples was the creation of London's sewer system in the early 1860s. One of the largest construction projects in world history up to that time, it fittingly used the new tools of industrialization to cure some of the ills of the industrial age.

Today it seems incredible that in the 1850s, London, a sprawling metropolis of some 2.5 million people, had no sewers. Instead, human and other wastes went into about two hundred thousand cesspools, underground pits that had to be emptied regularly. This job had long been done by so-called night-soil men. They hauled the sewage away to farms and other areas outside the city. But over time, as London's population soared, they could no longer keep up with demand, and many cesspools began to overflow. "Their contents were allowed to ooze through the floorboards or cracks in the walls," as one modern observer says, "and flow at random through yards and ditches, fouling everything they touched."[44]

The resulting unsanitary conditions were appalling and contributed to the spread of disease. In 1854 a series of cholera epidemics struck London, killing as many as thirty thousand people, ten times the number that died in the U.S. 9/11 attacks in 2001. Some of the survivors in a poor neighborhood addressed the government in a letter to the *Times* of London, saying:

May we beg and beseech your pro-teckshion and power [because] we live in muck and filth. We ain't got no priviz [toilets], no dust bins, [no] water-splies, and no drain or suer in the hole place. . . . The [stench] is disgustin. We all of us suffer, and numbers are ill, and if the Colera comes Lord help us.[45]

More such pleas, along with many complaints, came as horrendous odors spread across the city. The "great stink," as it was called, became so unbearable in 1858 that Parliament felt compelled to act. The government hired civil engineer Joseph Bazalgette (1819–1891) to construct a sewer system in London.

Bazalgette, who had trained with noted engineer John MacNeill (creator of extensive railroads in Ireland), wasted no time. He designed an elaborate underground tunnel network intended to neatly carry away almost all of London's sewage to the Thames Estuary, downstream from the city. Starting in 1859, in a little more than five years a sewer system of staggering size and complexity took shape. It contained six main arteries that totaled 100 miles (161km) in length; these alone required 318 million bricks and 880,000 cubic yards (670,000 cubic m) of concrete and mortar. From these main sewers branched 450 miles (720km) of somewhat narrower tunnels, which in turn branched out into some 13,000 miles (21,000km) of small local sewers. A newspaper, the *Observer*, called it "the most extensive and wonderful work of modern times."[46]

The Crystal Palace and Great Exhibition

That British engineers and workmen could build such an immense and complicated structure came as no surprise to people in other nations. Only a few years before, Britain had boldly demonstrated its status as the world's

British engineer Isambard Kingdom Brunel was one of several engineers who helped construct the Crystal Palace, home to the first world's fair (or Great Exhibition as it was called in 1851). Here, he stands in front of the chains of his Great Eastern steamship.

Eyewitness to the Crystal Palace

Among the many visitors to the Crystal Palace was the famous English novelist Charlotte Brontë (author of Jane Eyre*). She penned the following description of her experience:*

Yesterday I went for the second time to the Crystal Palace. We remained in it about three hours, and I must say I was more struck with it on this occasion than at my first visit. It is a wonderful place—vast, strange, new, and impossible to describe. Its grandeur does not consist in one thing, but in the unique assemblage of all things. Whatever human industry has created you find there, from the great compartments filled with railway engines and boilers, with mill machinery in full work, with splendid carriages of all kinds, with harness of every description, to the glass-covered and velvet-spread stands loaded with the most gorgeous work of the goldsmith and silversmith, and the carefully guarded caskets full of real diamonds and pearls worth hundreds of thousands of pounds. . . . It seems as if only magic could have gathered this mass of wealth from all the ends of the earth.

Quoted in *MyTimemachine,* "Eyewitness: The Great Exhibition, 1851." www.mytimemachine.co.uk/great exhibition.htm.

The Crystal Palace was designed by Joseph Paxton to showcase British inventions for the Great Exhibition of 1851. The palace was mostly of prefabricated materials like iron girders and large glass panels, making it easy to build and dismantle.

industrial leader. In 1851 London's Hyde Park hosted the Great Exhibition of the Works of Industry of All Nations, then, as now, recognized as the first ever world's fair. True to its name, the exhibition housed inventions and other exhibits from around the globe. However, the majority of the exhibits were products of British ingenuity and manufacturing. On display were ironworks and demonstrations of iron-smelting, steam hammers and a steam-powered tractor, advanced cannons and other firearms, the newest tools and kitchen appliances, and all manner of machines. There were some fourteen thousand exhibits in all, and the exhibition drew more than 6.2 million visitors, then viewed as a stupendous success.

The most impressive industrial creation of all was the gigantic building that housed the exhibits. Made up almost entirely of iron girders and large glass panels, it was appropriately dubbed the Crystal Palace. It measured an astounding 1,850 feet (564m) long, 110 feet (33m) high, and covered 25 acres (10ha). The building not only foreshadowed the widespread use of iron girders and glass seen in the twentieth century, it also showed the great usefulness of prefabricated (or prefab) materials; that is, premade, mass-produced construction units. (Mass production had long before become a hallmark of the Industrial Revolution. What was new was its application to large-scale building.) Utilizing many prefab units, the Crystal Palace had taken only nine

months to erect. Moreover, it could be easily dismantled and moved. In fact, it was moved to a new location a few years after the Great Exhibition closed. The building was finally destroyed by fire in 1936.

Most responsible for this marvel of the age were architect Joseph Paxton (1803–1865) and engineer William Cubitt (1785–1861). However, out of pride in their nation and its achievements, many other British engineers and builders worked on the Crystal Palace or other features of the Great Exhibition. Among them, not surprisingly, was Brunel, who was already in the early planning stages for his *Great Eastern*.

Unlike many of his colleagues, Brunel was not worried about foreign engineers, inventors, and machinists coming to the exhibition to copy British ideas and devices. He was certain that Britain would long remain the strongest nation on earth with by far the largest industrial base and economy. As one modern scholar puts it, "The British lead in textiles, metallurgy, mining, and machine building seemed insurmountable."[47] Also, Brunel was known for his disdain for patents and secrecy and his willingness to share ideas and credit for projects and inventions with others. "Most good things are being thought of by many persons at the same time," he famously said. "If there were publicity and freedom of communication, instead of concealment and mystery, a hundred times as many useful ideas would be generated."[48]

A Host of Engineering Marvels   81

Although there was a measure of truth in this statement, Brunel was dead wrong about Britain retaining its vast lead in industrial innovation and output. Not long after the Great Exhibition's doors had closed, that lead began to shrink. In an amazingly short span of time, U.S. industrial invention and production outstripped that of Britain. The so-called Second Industrial Revolution in America was destined to transform its makers and the world even more than the first.

Epilogue

THE DECLINE OF
BRITISH INDUSTRY

The Industrial Revolution had begun in Britain, and the British long led the world in industrial innovation and output. Yet in a relatively short time span in the late nineteenth and early twentieth centuries, Britain rapidly lost it lead in these areas to competitor nations, especially the United States and Germany. For example, the British iron and steel industries fell behind those of the United States and Germany in the 1890s. And by 1910 the United States produced almost twice as much steel as Britain did. Also, by 1913 Britain produced only 11 percent of the world's chemicals, compared to 34 percent for the United States and 24 percent for Germany. More and more, other industrial nations were able to surpass Britain in industrial ingenuity and achievement.

A Loss of Competitiveness

The reasons for this decline of British industry are many, complex, and still hotly debated by scholars. But most experts agree about a few crucial trends and developments that played major roles in the decline.

First, British businessmen and industrialists failed to keep up with and adopt new technology that emerged in the mid- to late nineteenth century. The machines that had driven the early decades of industry in Britain were mainly very simple forms of technology. Most, including looms with multiple spindles, the steam engine, and railways, were clever elaborations of devices and processes that had been around for a long time. Only in the nineteenth century did more advanced technologies based on discoveries in chemistry, physics, optics, and other sciences emerge.

The British iron and steel industries fell behind those of the United States in the 1890s. Large industrial steel mills, like the one pictured here, flourished in states such as Pennsylvania in the twentieth century.

Industrialists in the United States, Germany, and elsewhere were quick to incorporate these new discoveries into their businesses. As Hobsbawm puts it, they accepted and readily drew upon a "consistent process of scientific experiment and testing for their" new machines and processes and forged "an increasingly close and continuous link between" themselves and "professional scientists and scientific institutions."[49]

By contrast, most of the captains of British industry did not follow this prudent route. Some may have been too complacent, assuming that the British industrial lead would continue because it was simply too huge to dent. Others apparently appreciated neither the importance of advancing science nor the enormous growth potential possessed by rivals like the United States. So the British invested too little in modernization, became less competitive, and steadily fell behind. Increasingly, wealthy British industrialists lived "off the remains of world monopoly [and the country's] past accumulations of wealth," Hobsbawm writes. "The difference between "the needs of modernization and the increasingly prosperous complacency of the rich grew ever more visible."[50]

A Failure of Education

At least as important, if not more so, in Britain's industrial decline was a failure of the country's educational system. In a nutshell, most of Britain's engineers and inventors learned in the apprentice system. And this system was ultimately unable to produce the number of qualified individuals needed to keep British industry up-to-date and competitive. In comparison, increasingly numerous formal engineering schools in France, the United Sates, Germany, and Japan did meet these needs.

Most engineers of the Industrial Revolution learned through an apprenticeship rather than at a university, which was one of several reasons Britain's industry declined. The University of Manchester (shown here) did not specialize in engineering like colleges in the United States and Germany.

Moreover, the British apprentice system produced few scientists; indeed, in the 1800s most residents of Britain of all classes were almost scientifically illiterate. One of those few scientists the system did produce, Lyon Playfair, recognized the problem, writing in 1852: "As surely as darkness follows the setting of the sun, so surely will England recede as a manufacturing nation, unless her industrial population becomes more conversant with science than they are now."[51] This prediction was fulfilled, much to Britain's disadvantage. By 1901, only half a century later, British colleges annually graduated only 3,000 students proficient in modern technologies; Germany turned out an impressive 10,700 per year, and the United States and Japan also surpassed Britain in this area.

Industry and the spread of new machines by no means stopped in Britain in the late 1800s. It remained an important manufacturing nation and a great power in world affairs. But its share of the global economic pie shrank considerably as the cutting edge of the Industrial Revolution shifted to other countries, especially the United States. In a parallel course, the British Empire would shrink, too, until, in a reversal of the old adage, the sun would once more begin to set each day on British soil.

Notes

Introduction: Why Eighteenth-Century Britain?

1. W.W. Rostow, *The Stages of Economic Growth*. New York: Cambridge University Press, 1991, p. 33.

Chapter One: The Rise of Industrial Britain

2. Kenneth O. Morgan, ed., *The Oxford Illustrated History of Britain*. New York: Oxford University Press, 2001, p. 419.
3. Quoted in Morgan, *The Oxford Illustrated History of Britain*, p. 420.
4. T.S. Ashton and Pat Hudson, *The Industrial Revolution, 1760–1830*. New York: Oxford University Press, 1998, p. 11.
5. Peter N. Stearns, *The Industrial Revolution in World History*. Boulder, CO: Westview, 2007, p. 5.
6. Mark Overton, "Agricultural Revolution in England 1500–1850," *British History*, BBC. www.bbc.co.uk/history/british/empire_seapower/agricultural_revolution_05.shtml.
7. Adam Smith, "Of the Division of Labor," in *An Inquiry into the Nature and Causes of the Wealth of Nations*, Book I (first published 1776); 5th ed., ed. Edwin Cannan. London: Methuen, 1904; repr., Library of Economics and Liberty, 2000. www.econlib.org/LIBRARY/Smith/smWN.html.
8. Crane Brinton et al., *A History of Civilization*. Englewood Cliffs, NJ: Prentice-Hall, 1995, p. 567.
9. Eric J. Hobsbawm and Chris Wrigley, *Industry and Empire: From 1750 to the Present Day*. New York: Norton, 1999, p. xi.
10. Stearns, *The Industrial Revolution in World History*, p. 5.
11. Brinton, *A History of Civilization*, p. 571.

Chapter Two: Textiles Lead the Way

12. Jeff Horn, *The Industrial Revolution*. Westport, CT: Greenwood, 2007, p. 34.
13. Hobsbawm and Wrigley, *Industry and Empire*, p. 34.
14. Hobsbawm and Wrigley, *Industry and Empire*, pp. 38–39.
15. Horn, *The Industrial Revolution*, p. 35.
16. Quoted in Stearns, *The Industrial Revolution in World History*, p. 23.
17. Horn, *The Industrial Revolution*, p. 66.

Chapter Three: Coal, Iron, and Steel

18. Horn, *The Industrial Revolution*, p. 40.
19. Quoted in Appalachian Blacksmiths Association, "Wrought Iron." www.appaltree.net/aba/education/historical/ironworks/ironworks6.htm.
20. Stearns, *The Industrial Revolution in World History*, p. 25.

Chapter Four: The Mainspring of Industry: Steam

21. Quoted in John Bowditch and Clement Ramsland, eds., *Voices of the Industrial Revolution*. Ann Arbor: University of Michigan Press, 1987, p. 129.
22. Andrew Ure, *The Philosophy of Manufactures*. New York: Burt Franklin, 1861, pp. 339–40.
23. Ashton and Hudson, *The Industrial Revolution, 1760–1830*, p. 29.
24. Quoted in H.W. Dickinson and Rhys Jenkins, *James Watt and the Steam Engine*. Oxford: Clarendon, 1927, p. 23.
25. Quoted in Brian Tierney and Joan Scott, eds., *Western Societies, a Documentary History*, vol. 2. New York: Knopf, 1984, pp. 140–43.

Chapter Five: Transportation and Communications

26. Ashton and Hudson, *The Industrial Revolution, 1760–1830*, p. 84.
27. Port Cities Southampton, "Steamship Pioneers," *The Blue Riband*. www.plimsoll.org/OnTheLine/TransatlanticTravel/TheBlueRiband/default.asp.
28. Quoted in J. Munro, *Heroes of the Telegraph*, Part 2, FullBooks.com. www.fullbooks.com/Heroes-of-the-Telegraph2.html.
29. Stearns, *The Industrial Revolution in World History*, p. 31.

Chapter Six: The Impact of Industrialization

30. Stearns, *The Industrial Revolution in World History*, p. 27.
31. Quoted in Laura L. Frader, *The Industrial Revolution: A History in Documents*. New York: Oxford University Press, 2006, pp. 61–62.
32. Quoted in Brinton, *A History of Civilization*, p. 572.
33. Brinton, *A History of Civilization*, p. 573.
34. John Stuart Mill, "The Remedies for Low Wages Further Considered," in *Principles of Political Economy with Some of Their Applications to Social Philosophy*, Book 2, (first published 1848); 7th ed., ed. W.J. Ashley. London: Longmans, Green, 1909; repr., Library of Economics and Liberty. www.econlib.org/library/Mill/mlP.html.
35. Quoted in G.D.H. Cole and A.W. Filson, eds., *British Working Class Movements: Selected Documents*. London: Macmillan, 1967, pp. 114–15.
36. Frader, *The Industrial Revolution: A History in Documents*, p. 97.

37. Horn, *The Industrial Revolution*, p. 119.

Chapter Seven: A Host of Engineering Marvels

38. Ashton and Hudson, *The Industrial Revolution, 1760–1830*, p. 81.
39. Quoted in Making the Modern World, "Inventing Engineering: What Makes an Engineer?" www.makingthemodernworld.org.uk/stories/manufacture_by_machine/02.ST.01/?scene=4.
40. Quoted in Deborah Cadbury, *Dreams of Iron and Steel: Seven Wonders of the Nineteenth Century*. New York: Fourth Estate, 2004, p. 3.
41. Quoted in Cadbury, *Dreams of Iron and Steel*, p. 1
42. Cadbury, *Dreams of Iron and Steel*, p. 1.
43. Quoted in Cadbury, *Dreams of Iron and Steel*, p. 31.
44. Cadbury, *Dreams of Iron and Steel*, p. 117.
45. Quoted in Leighton Carter, "The Slum of All Fears," Victorian Web. www.victorianweb.org/authors/dickens/bleakhouse/carter.html.
46. Quoted in Cadbury, *Dreams of Iron and Steel*, p. 115.
47. Stearns, *The Industrial Revolution in World History*, p. 43.
48. Quoted in John Dugan, "The Engineers and the Crystal Palace," Victorian Web. www.victorianweb.org/history/1851/engineers.html.

Epilogue: The Decline of British Industry

49. Hobsbawm and Wrigley, *Industry and Empire*, p. 151.
50. Hobsbawm and Wrigley, *Industry and Empire*, p. 170.
51. Quoted in Making the Modern World, "Inventing Engineering: The Emerging Crisis." www.makingthemodernworld.org.uk/stories/manufacture_by_machine/02.ST.01/?scene=6.

Time Line

1712
Englishman Thomas Newcomen creates the first commercially successful steam engine.

1756
The Seven Years' War begins in Europe.

1761
Engineer Thomas Brindley completes the Bridgewater Canal in western England.

1765
The introduction of the spinning jenny begins to revolutionize the textile industry.

1770
English explorer James Cook claims Australia for Britain.

1775
Scotsman James Watt introduces a steam engine more efficient than Newcomen's.

1776
British economist Adam Smith publishes *The Wealth of Nations*; England's thirteen American colonies declare their independence.

1779
Samuel Compton introduces the "spinning mule," which produces thread much faster than an ordinary spinning wheel.

1789
The French Revolution begins.

1800–1820
In England, the Luddites, workers opposed to industrialization, attack factories.

1810
In South America, Argentina gains its independence.

1815
French dictator Napoléon Bonaparte is defeated at Waterloo; Britain now makes half of all the world's manufactured goods.

1821
English chemist Michael Faraday demonstrates the principle of the electric motor.

1830
In England, railroad service begins between London and Liverpool.

1831
Faraday discovers electromagnetic current, making electric signals possible.

1843
The first large iron steamship, the *Great Britain*, is launched.

1850

The population of industrial Britain reaches 16.6 million.

1851

Britain shows off its industrial prowess in London's Great Exhibition, the first world's fair.

1856

Henry Bessemer introduces the Bessemer Converter, which increases the speed and volume of steel production.

1857

In India, the Sepoys, Indian soldiers loyal to Britain, rebel against the British.

1861–1865

The United States and Confederacy fight the American Civil War.

1866

The first permanent, successful transatlantic cable links England with North America.

1870–1871

The Franco-Prussian War rocks Europe.

1890

The Forth Bridge, the world's first all-steel bridge, is completed in Scotland.

1910

With British industry in decline, the United States now produces twice as much steel as Britain each year.

For More Information

Books

T.S. Ashton and Pat Hudson, *The Industrial Revolution, 1760–1830*. New York: Oxford University Press, 1998. An excellent general look at the early years of the Industrial Revolution. Hudson, an economic historian, provides commentary updating Ashton's classic 1949 book.

Deborah Cadbury, *Dreams of Iron and Steel: Seven Wonders of the Nineteenth Century*. New York: Fourth Estate, 2004. Examines several megaprojects made possible by industrialization, including the Panama Canal, Brooklyn Bridge, and London's sewers.

Laura L. Frader, *The Industrial Revolution: A History in Documents*. New York: Oxford University Press, 2006. One of the best collections of primary sources for the Industrial Revolution.

E.J. Hobsbawm and Chris Wrigley, *Industry and Empire: From 1750 to the Present Day*. New York: Norton, 1999. Looks at how large-scale industrialization facilitated the rise of imperial Britain. Highly recommended.

Jeff Horn, *The Industrial Revolution*. Westport, CT: Greenwood, 2007. A useful discussion of the Industrial Revolution, concentrating especially on global trade and other economic developments.

Charles More, *Understanding the Industrial Revolution*. London: Routledge, 2000. A clearly written volume that makes the Industrial Revolution accessible to nonscholars.

Kenneth Morgan, *The Birth of Industrial Britain*. London: Longman, 1999. A well-researched overview of the subject.

———, ed., *The Oxford Illustrated History of Britain*. New York: Oxford University Press, 2001. A useful examination of British history that provides context for the rise of industry in the 1700s and 1800s.

Patrick O'Brien and Roland Quinault, eds., *The Industrial Revolution and British Society*. Cambridge: Cambridge University Press, 1993. A very well-written account of how the Industrial Revolution affected society.

Kirkpatrick Sale, *Rebels Against the Future: The Luddites and Their War on the Industrial Revolution*. Cambridge, MA: Perseus, 1996. This eye-opening volume examines the extreme negative reactions of some people in Britain to ongoing industrialization. Highly recommended.

Peter N. Stearns, *The Industrial Revolution in World History*. Boulder, CO: Westview, 2007. A good, straightforward look at the Industrial Revolution and how it changed the world.

Peter N. Stearns and John H. Hinshaw, *The ABC-CLIO World History Companion to the Industrial Revolution*. Santa Barbara, CA: ABC-CLIO, 1996. A useful collection of short articles about numerous aspects of the Industrial Revolution.

Web Resources

The Agricultural Revolution in England 1500–1850 (www.bbc.co.uk/history/british/empire_seapower/agricultural_revolution_05.shtml). A scholar explores the changes in agriculture that helped to pave the way for the onset of the Industrial Revolution.

The Industrial Revolution: An Overview, The Victorian Web (www.victorianweb.org/technology/ir/irov.html). An excellent compilation of short articles on Industrial Revolution topics, including textiles, railroads, inventors, engineers, a chronology, and much more.

Internet Modern History Sourcebook: The Industrial Revolution (www.fordham.edu/halsall/mod/modsbook14.html). A very useful collection of articles on the Industrial Revolution, including several on its social, political, and urban effects.

Subterranea Britannica: "The Tower Subway" (www.subbrit.org.uk/sb-sites/sites/t/tower_subway/index.shtml). An information-packed, nicely illustrated article about the building of the Tower Subway in London, one of the great engineering projects of the Industrial Revolution.

Index

A

Agriculture
    advances in, 16, 18
    enclosure and, 16–17
    preindustrial, 15–16
Apprentice system, 72–74, 86
Archimedes, 9
Arkwright, Richard, 25, 27, 28, 29
Ashton, T.S., 15, 56
Automobile, 51, *51*

B

Bazalgette, Joseph, 78
Bessemer, Henry, 39, 40
Bessemer converter, *39*, 40
Blaenavon Ironworks (Wales), *34*
Blast furnace, *36*
Bloye, William, 12
Boulton, Matthew, *12*, 48
Bridgewater Canal, 54
Brindley, James, 54
Brinton, Crane, 20–21
Brontë, Charlotte, 80
Brunel, Isambard K., 74, 75–76, *76*, *79*, 81–82
Brunel, Marc I., 74

C

Cadbury, Deborah, 77
Canals, 53–54
Capitalists, 62
Cartwright, Edmund, 29
Charlotte Dundas (steamboat), 58
Child labor, *63*
Cholera epidemics, 78
Clifton Suspension Bridge, 75

Coal/coal production, 41–42
    link with iron production, 33
Coke, 35
A Compendius History of the Cotton Manufacture (Guest), 49–50
Compton, Samuel, 29
Cooke, William, 60
Cooper, Thomas, 30
Cort, Henry, 35
Cotton mills, 28
    child labor in, *63*
    working conditions in, 64
Cromford Mill, *28*, 30
Crystal Palace, 80, 81
Ctesibius, 9, 10
Cubitt, William, 81
Cugnot, Nicholas, 51

D

Darby, Abraham, 35, 36
Davy, Humphry, 41
Dickens, Charles, 49

E

Eads Bridge (St. Louis), 41
Economist (magazine), 75
Edinburgh Review (newspaper), 14
Egerton, Francis, 54
Electric motors, 59

F

Factories/factory system, 31–32
    first modern-style, 28
    workers' protests against, 67–69
Faraday, Michael, 59
Flying shuttle, *26*, 26–27

G

Gaskell, Peter, 15
The Golden Boys (Bloye), 12
Gramme, Zénobe, 60
Grand Trunk Canal (Trent and Mersey Canal), 54, *54*, 56
Great Britain (steamship), 75
Great Eastern (steamship), 75–77, *76*
Great Exhibition of the Works of Industry of All Nations (1851), 81
Great Western Railway, 75
Greathead, James H., 74
Guest, Richard, 49–50

H

Hard Times (Dickens), 49
Hargreaves, James, 25, 27
Hero (Heron), 9
Highs, Thomas, 25
Hobsbawm, Eric J., 21, 25, 85
Horn, Jeff, 18, 24–25, 32, 71
Horse-power, 43
Howe, Elias, 29
Hunt, Walter, 29
Huntsman, Benjamin, 38

I

Industrial Revolution
    Britain loses lead in, 83–86
    environmental impacts of, 64
    societal impacts of, 21–22, 62–64, 65–67
    spread of, 69, 71
Iron bridge, first, 37, *37*
Iron plow, 16
Iron production
    innovations in, 35–38
    link with coal, 33–34
Iron rails, 56

K
Kay, John, 25, 26–27

L
Labor/trade unions, 67, 68–69
L'Ecole Royale des Ponts et
    Chaussées, 72
Liverpool and Manchester
    Railway, 55
Locomotives, 56–57
    first steam, *50, 52*
Luddites, 67
    loyalty oath of, 69

M
MacNeill, John, 78
Manufacturing
    preindustrial, 15
    transition from manual to
        machine, 19–20
Martin, Pierre-Émile, 40
Middle class, rise of, 22
Mill, John Stuart, 67
Millwrights, 73
Morgan, Kenneth O., 14
Murdoch, William, *12,* 48
Murray, Matthew, 57

N
Newcomen, Thomas, 41, 45

O
Observer (newspaper), 78
Owen, Robert, 30–31, *31,* 43, 67

P
Paul, Lewis, 27
Paxton, Joseph, 81
Playfair, Lyon, 86
Power loom, 29
Pritchard, Thomas F., 37

R
Railroads, 56–57
    first passenger, 55, *55*
    in Russia, 70

steam-powered locomotive
    and, *50,* 52
Rennie, George, 55
Rennie, John, 55
Rocket (steam locomotive), 55,
    57
Roller spinning machine, 27
Rostow, W.W., 11, 13
Russia, 70

S
Savery, Thomas, 46
Seed drill, 16, *17*
Sewer system, 77–78
Sewing machines, 29
Siemens, Carl W., 40
Singer, Isaac M., 29
Sirius (steamboat), *58, 59*
Slavery, in Greece, 11
Smiles, Samuel, 65
Smith, Adam, 19–20
Social change, 21–22, 62–64,
    65–67
Spinning jenny, 27
Spinning mule, 29
Steam engine, 43–45, *44*
    first, 9
    first auto powered by, 51, *51*
    high-pressure, 52
    Watt's improvement on,
        46, 48
Steamboats, 58–59
Strearns, Peter N., 16, 21, 63
Steel production, 38–41
Stephenson, George, 57, *73*
Stephenson, Robert, 55, 57

T
Telegraph, 59, 60
    first transatlantic cable for,
        60, 61
Textile industry
    cotton, 23–25
    factory system develops in,
        30–32
    mechanization of, 25–27, 29

steam engine and, 49–50
    See also Cotton mills
Textile mill, *24*
Thames Tunnel, 74
Threshing machine, 16
Times of London (newspaper),
    61, 78
Towns, 20
    living/working conditions
        in, 22, 64
Trans-Siberian Railway, 70, *70*
Trent and Mersey Canal
    (Grand Trunk Canal), 54,
    54, 56
Trevithick, Richard, 52, 56–57
Tull, Jethro, 16, 17
Tunnels, 74–75

U
University of Manchester, *85*
Ure, Andrew, 43–44

V
Vitruvius, 10
Volta, Alessandro, 59
Voltaic pile, 59

W
Water frame, 27, 29
Water pump
    of Ctesibius, 10
    steam driven, 45–46
Watt, James, *12,* 45, *46,* 48
Wealth of Nations (Smith), 19
Wheatstone, Charles, 60
Whitney, Eli, 29
Wilkinson, John, 36–38, 48
Workers
    argument for better
        conditions for, 66–67
    conditions for, 63–64
    exploitation of, 65
    in factory system, 31–32
    impact of farming advances
        on, 17, 19
Wyatt, John, 27

Picture Credits

About the Author

In addition to his acclaimed volumes on the ancient world, historian Don Nardo has written and edited many books for young adults about modern European and American history, including *The Age of Colonialism*, *The French Revolution*, *The Atlantic Slave Trade*, *The Declaration of Independence*, *The Great Depression*, and *World War II in the Pacific*. Nardo also writes screenplays and teleplays and composes music. He lives with his wife, Christine, in Massachusetts.